MW01234786

Breville Smart Air Fryer Cookbook for Beginners

2000+ Days of Effortless Recipes for Chef Quality Breakfasts, Lunches and Dinners with Your Breville Air Fryer Oven

Gina Petite

Table of Contents

Introduction

Are you looking for a new smart Air Fryer oven that will help you cook all sorts of meals? Well, you are about to get lucky, as we are introducing you to the amazing Breville Smart Air Fryer Oven. We all know Breville due to its variety of kitchen appliances. From the first toasted, they presented to the latest Air Fryer ovens; all came with quality and durability offered by Breville. As of today, there is a range of innovations that Breville introduced in the tech world. The smartest Breville Smart Air Fryer Oven is proven to be the most successful model of this range due to its smart features. In this air fryer oven cookbook, you can learn all about the Breville smart Air Fryer Oven and will get to know various recipes that you can cook using its smart cooking functions.

Benefits of Using Breville Smart Air Fryer Oven

1. *Space Friendly Design:*

The design of the Air Fryer oven is something that makes it stand out among the rest of the air fryer ovens in the market. It's size and shape make a complete balance; you can manage cooking space and your countertop space at the same time. Since this oven can replace multiple food appliances due to a variety of its cooking functions, it can be easily placed and set anywhere in the kitchen.

2. *13 Cooking Functions:*

This one appliance can replace most of the cooking appliances in your kitchen as it provides a number of cooking functions in one place. This Air Fryer oven can be used to bake food, toast, grill, roast, cookies, broil, and dehydrate all sorts of food items. The versatility of its cooking function increases when you count the temperature and timer settings, which can also be adjusted manually to cook according to your own preferences. There are several accessories that come

with the oven, and they all help to cook on a specific cooking mode.

3. *Large Capacity:*

The Breville Air fryer oven is known for its large size and all the capacity suitable for cooking all portion sizes. So, whether you have one large family or a small family, this Air fryer oven can serve the needs of all. Now baking a 14 pounds turkey and roasting a whole chicken or a duck is not a problem, as you can not only adjust them all in this Air Fryer oven, but you can also add side ingredients along with them.

4. *Smart Control Panel and Crisping Technology:*

Another good feature of this Air Fryer oven is its easy and simple control panel, which is completely user friendly. The control dial is used to select the mode of cooking in each option.

Breville Smart Air Fryer Oven Deconstructed

When you unbox the appliance, you will find the following parts and components inside:

- The main cooking unit
- Air fry basket
- Baking dish
- Wire rack
- Crumb tray
- Dehydrator tray

All these accessories are dishwasher safe, can be removed and washed after the cooking session.

Control Panel and Cooking Functions:

The control panel is fixed on the front of the appliance, on top. And it has a dial, five buttons, and a display screen. On this screen, you can see all the presets written on the screen indicating different cooking functions:

- Bagel
- Toast
- Air fry
- Bake
- Roast
- Broil
- Cookies
- Pizza
- Reheat

How to use Breville Smart Air Fryer Oven

Here are a few simple steps to use your Breville Smart Air Fryer Oven:

1. *Getting Started:*

At first, place the appliance at an appropriate place in the kitchen. The back and top of the oven should be kept open for ventilation. Check all its accessories and then plug it in. The lights of the display screen will light up.

If you are using the oven for the first time, make sure to wash all the accessories with water or soap water and allow them to dry, and keep them at a place where they are safe from the dirt and grease.

2. *Setting Up the oven:*

The crumb tray is placed at the bottom of the oven, and it is important to use this tray to protect the floor of the oven. So always fix the crumb tray in the lowermost portion of the oven. You can now select the accessories according to the recipe and the type of food. The air fryer basket is used to Air Fry a variety of food items, so use this basket to keep the food inside the oven.

3. *Cooking and Adjustment:*

Now that you have selected the desired accessories for cooking. Prepare your food and keep it ready for the oven. The oven quickly attains the required heat for cooking, so it is suggested not to preheat the oven and directly place the food inside and then select the cooking functions. You can then adjust the settings according to the given recipe. Generally, it is best to select after your food is placed inside.

Cleaning and Maintenance

Unplug the appliance and remove all the trays or pans placed inside. Make sure to wear gloves or oven mittens while handling the hot trays. It is important to clean the tray and pan while they are hot to prevent all the grease and food particles stuck on them from hardening.

1. Leave the cooking appliance with its door open and allow it to cool completely.
2. Use this time to wash all the accessories used in the cooking operation. You can either wash them by lightly rub them with soap water or wash them in the dishwasher. Avoid using hard material to scrub these accessories, as they could damage their outer surface.
3. Now that the oven is cooled from inside out, you can take a lightly damp cloth and wipe off all the grease and food particles from the inner walls of the Air Fryer oven.
4. Use another lightly wet cloth to wipe off the doors, door handle, the control panel dial, its buttons, and the displace screen.
5. Never immerse the unit water and keep it away from liquids as well.

Breville Video Tutorial
https://www.youtube.com/@breville/videos

Breakfast Recipes

Oats, Nuts & Seeds Granola

Servings: 8
Preparation Time: 15 minutes
Cooking Time: 15 minutes

Ingredients:

- 1/3 cup olive oil
- ¼ cup maple syrup
- 2 tablespoons honey
- ½ teaspoon vanilla extract
- 2 cups rolled oats
- ½ cup wheat germ, toasted
- ¼ cup dried cherries
- ¼ cup dried blueberries
- 2 tablespoons dried cranberries
- 2 tablespoons sunflower seeds
- 2 tablespoons pumpkin seeds, shelled
- 1 tablespoon flax seed
- 2 tablespoons pecans, chopped
- 2 tablespoons hazelnuts, chopped
- 2 tablespoons almonds, chopped
- 2 tablespoons walnuts, chopped
- ½ teaspoon ground cinnamon
- 1/8 t teaspoon ground cloves

Instructions:

1. In a small bowl, add the oil and maple syrup and mix well.
2. In a large bowl, add the remaining ingredients and mix well.
3. Add the oil mixture and mix until well combined.
4. Place the mixture into a baking dish.
5. Select "Air Fry" of Breville Smart Air Fryer Oven and adjust the temperature to 350 degrees F.
6. Set the timer for 15 minutes and press "Start/Stop" to begin preheating.
7. When the unit beeps to show that it is preheated, arrange the baking dish over the wire rack.
8. While cooking, stir the granola after every 5 minutes.
9. When the cooking time is complete, remove the baking dish from the oven.
10. Set the granola aside to cool completely before serving.

Dried Fruit Oatmeal

Servings: 8
Preparation Time: 10 minutes
Cooking Time: 8 hours

Ingredients:

- 2 cups steel-cut oats
- 1/3 cup dried apricots, chopped
- 1/3 cup raisins
- 1/3 cup dried cherries
- 1 teaspoon ground cinnamon
- 6 cups water
- 4 cups milk
- 4 cups water
- ¼ teaspoon liquid stevia

Instructions:

1. In an oven-safe pan that will fit in the Breville Smart Air Fryer Oven, place all ingredients and stir to combine.
2. Cover the pan with a lid.
3. Arrange the pan over the wire rack.
4. Select "Slow Cooker" of Breville Smart Air Fryer Oven and set on "Low".
5. Set the timer for 8 hours and press "Start/Stop" to begin cooking.
6. When the cooking time is complete, remove the pan from the oven.
7. Remove the lid and stir the mixture well.
8. Serve warm.

Cinnamon French Toasts

Servings: 2
Preparation Time: 10 minutes
Cooking Time: 5 minutes

Ingredients:

- 2 eggs
- ¼ cup whole milk
- 3 tablespoons sugar
- 2 teaspoons olive oil

- 1/8 teaspoon vanilla extract
- 1/8 teaspoon ground cinnamon
- 4 bread slices

Instructions:

1. In a large bowl, add all the ingredients except for bread slices and beat until well combined.
2. Coat the bread slices with egg mixture evenly.
3. Arrange the bread slices in the air fry basket.
4. Select "Air Fry" of Breville Smart Air Fryer Oven and adjust the temperature to 390 degrees F.
5. Set the timer for 5 minutes and press "Start/Stop" to begin preheating.
6. When the unit beeps to show that it is preheated, insert the air fry basket in the oven.
7. Flip the bread slices once halfway through.
8. When the cooking time is complete, remove the air fry basket from the oven.
9. Serve warm.

Cheddar Mustard Toasts

Servings: 2
Preparation Time: 10 minutes
Cooking Time: 10 minutes

Ingredients:

- 4 bread slices
- 2 tablespoons cheddar cheese, shredded
- 2 eggs, whites and yolks, separated
- 1 tablespoon mustard
- 1 tablespoon paprika

Instructions:

1. In a clean glass bowl, add the egg whites in and beat until they form soft peaks.
2. In another bowl, mix together the cheese, egg yolks, mustard, and paprika.
3. Gently fold in the egg whites.

Parmesan Eggs in Avocado Cups

Servings: 2
Preparation Time: 10 minutes
Cooking Time: 12 minutes

4. Spread the mustard mixture over the toasted bread slices.
5. Arrange the bread slices in the air fry basket.
6. Select "Air Fry" of Breville Smart Air Fryer Oven and adjust the temperature to 355 degrees F.
7. Set the timer for 10 minutes and press "Start/Stop" to begin preheating.
8. When the unit beeps to show that it is preheated, insert the air fry basket in the oven.
9. When the cooking time is complete, remove the air fry basket from the oven.
10. Serve warm.

Cheese Toasts with Bacon

Servings: 2
Preparation Time: 10 minutes
Cooking Time: 4 minutes

Ingredients:

- 4 bread slices
- 1 garlic clove, minced
- 4 ounces goat cheese, crumbled
- Freshly ground black pepper, to taste
- 8 cooked bacon slices, crumbled

Instructions:

1. In a food processor, add the garlic, ricotta, lemon zest and black pepper and pulse until smooth.
2. Spread ricotta mixture over each bread slices evenly.
3. Arrange the bread slices in the air fry basket.
4. Select "Air Fry" of Breville Smart Air Fryer Oven and adjust the temperature to 355 degrees F.
5. Set the timer for 4 minutes and press "Start/Stop" to begin preheating.
6. When the unit beeps to show that it is preheated, insert the air fry basket in the oven.
7. When the cooking time is complete, remove the air fry basket from the oven and transfer the bread slices onto serving plates.
8. Top with bacon pieces and serv

Ingredients:

- 1 avocado, halved and pitted
- Salt and ground black pepper, as required
- 2 eggs

- 1 tablespoon Parmesan cheese, shredded

Instructions:

1. Arrange a greased square piece of foil in the air fry basket.
2. Select "Bake" of Breville Smart Air Fryer Oven and adjust the temperature to 390 degrees F.
3. Set the timer for 12 minutes and press "Start/Stop" to begin preheating.
4. Meanwhile, carefully scoop out about 2 teaspoons of flesh from each avocado half.
5. Crack 1 egg in each avocado half and sprinkle with salt, black pepper and cheese.

9. When the unit beeps to show that it is preheated, arrange the avocado halves into the prepared air fry basket and insert in the oven.
10. When the cooking time is complete, transfer the avocado halves onto serving plates.
11. Top with Parmesan and serve.

Eggs in Bread Cups

Servings: 4
Preparation Time: 10 minutes
Cooking Time: 23 minutes

Ingredients:

- 4 bacon slices
- 2 bread slices, crust removed
- 4 eggs
- Salt and ground black pepper, as required

Instructions:

1. Grease 4 cups of the muffin tin and set aside.
2. Heat a small frying pan over medium-high heat and cook the bacon slices for about 2-3 minutes.
3. With a slotted spoon, transfer the bacon slice onto a paper towel-lined plate to cool.
4. Break each bread slice in half.
5. Arrange 1 bread slice half in each of the prepared muffin cups and press slightly.
6. Now, arrange 1 bacon slice over each bread slice in a circular shape.
7. Crack 1 egg into each muffin cup and sprinkle with salt and black pepper.

8. Select "Bake" of Breville Smart Air Fryer Oven and adjust the temperature to 350 degrees F.
9. Set the timer for 20 minutes and press "Start/Stop" to begin preheating.
10. When the unit beeps to show that it is preheated, arrange the muffin tin over the wire rack.
11. When the cooking time is complete, remove the muffin tin from the oven.
12. Serve warm.

Eggs in Bread & Bacon Cups

Servings: 4
Preparation Time: 10 minutes
Cooking Time: 15 minutes

Ingredients:

- 4 bacon slices
- 4 bread slices
- 1 scallion, chopped
- 2 tablespoons bell pepper, seeded and chopped
- 1½ tablespoons mayonnaise
- 4 eggs

Instructions:

1. Grease 6 cups of the muffin tin.
2. Line the sides of each prepared muffin cup with 1 bacon slice.
3. Cut bread slices with a round cookie cutter.
4. Arrange the bread slice in the bottom of each muffin cup.
5. Top with scallion, bell pepper and mayonnaise evenly.
6. Carefully crack one egg in each muffin cup.
7. Select "Air Fry" of Breville Smart Air Fryer Oven and adjust the temperature to 375 degrees F.
8. Set the timer for 15 minutes and press "Start/Stop" to begin preheating.
9. When the unit beeps to show that it is preheated, arrange the muffin tin over the wire rack.
10. When the cooking time is complete, remove the muffin tin from the oven.
11. Serve warm.

Baked Eggs

Servings: 4
Preparation Time: 10 minutes
Cooking Time: 12 minutes

Ingredients:

- 1 cup marinara sauce, divided
- 1 tablespoon capers, drained and divided
- 8 eggs
- ¼ cup whipping cream, divided
- ¼ cup Parmesan cheese, shredded and divided
- Salt and ground black pepper, as required

Instructions:

1. Grease 4 ramekins. Set aside.
2. Divide the marinara sauce in the bottom of each prepared ramekin evenly and top with capers.
3. Carefully crack 2 eggs over marinara sauce into each ramekin and top with cream, followed by the Parmesan cheese.
4. Sprinkle each ramekin with salt and black pepper.
5. Select "Bake" of Breville Smart Air Fryer Oven and adjust the temperature to 400 degrees F.
6. Set the timer for 12 minutes and press "Start/Stop" to begin preheating.
7. When the unit beeps to show that it is preheated, arrange the ramekins over the wire rack.
8. When the cooking time is complete, remove the ramekins from the oven.
9. Serve warm.

Egg & Spinach Tart

Servings: 4
Preparation Time: 15 minutes
Cooking Time: 25 minutes

Ingredients:

- 1 puff pastry sheet, trimmed into a 9x13-inch rectangle
- 4 eggs
- ½ cup cheddar cheese, grated
- 7 cooked thick-cut bacon strips
- ½ cup cooked spinach
- 1 egg, lightly beaten

Instructions:

1. Arrange the pastry in a lightly greased enamel roasting pan.
2. With a small knife gently, cut a 1-inch border around the edges of the puff pastry without cutting all the way through.
3. With a fork, pierce the center of the pastry a few times.
4. Select "Bake" of Breville Smart Air Fryer Oven and adjust the temperature to 400 degrees F.
5. Set the timer for 10 minutes and press "Start/Stop" to begin preheating.
6. When the unit beeps to show that it is preheated, insert the roasting pan in the oven.
7. When the cooking time is complete, remove the roasting pan from the oven and sprinkle the cheese over the center.
8. Place the spinach and bacon in an even layer across the tart.
9. Now, crack the eggs, leaving space between each one.
10. Select "Bake" of Breville Smart Air Fryer Oven and adjust the temperature to 400 degrees F.
11. Set the timer for 15 minutes and press "Start/Stop" to begin preheating.
12. Insert the roasting pan in the oven.
13. When the cooking time is complete, remove the roasting pan from the oven and set aside to cool for 2-3 minutes before cutting.
14. With a pizza cutter, cut into 4 portions and serve.

Cheddar & Cream Omelet

Servings: 2
Preparation Time: 10 minutes
Cooking Time: 8 minutes

Ingredients:

- 4 eggs
- ¼ cup cream
- Salt and ground black pepper, as required
- ¼ cup Cheddar cheese, grated

Instructions:

1. In a bowl, add the eggs, cream, salt, and black pepper and beat well.
2. Place the egg mixture into a small baking dish.

3. Select "Air Fry" of Breville Smart Air Fryer Oven and adjust the temperature to 350 degrees F.
4. Set the timer for 8 minutes and press "Start/Stop" to begin preheating.
5. When the unit beeps to show that it is preheated, arrange the baking dish over the wire rack.
6. After 4 minutes of cooking, sprinkle the omelet with cheese evenly.
7. When the cooking time is complete, remove the baking dish from oven.
8. Cut the omelet into 2 portions and serve hot.

Bell Pepper Omelet

Servings: 2
Preparation Time: 10 minutes
Cooking Time: 10 minutes

Ingredients:

- 1 teaspoon butter
- 1 small onion, sliced
- ½ of green bell pepper, seeded and chopped
- 4 eggs
- ¼ teaspoon milk
- Salt and ground black pepper, as required
- ¼ cup Cheddar cheese, grated

Instructions:

1. In a skillet, melt the butter over medium heat and cook the onion and bell pepper for about 4-5 minutes.
2. Remove the skillet from heat and set aside to cool slightly.
3. Meanwhile, in a bowl, add the eggs, milk, salt and black pepper and beat well.
4. Add the cooked onion mixture and gently stir to combine.
5. Place the bell pepper mixture into a small baking dish.
6. Select "Air Fry" of Breville Smart Air Fryer Oven and adjust the temperature to 355 degrees F.
7. Set the timer for 10 minutes and press "Start/Stop" to begin preheating.
8. When the unit beeps to show that it is preheated, arrange the baking dish over the wire rack.
9. When the cooking time is complete, remove the baking dish from oven and place onto a wire rack to cool for about 5 minutes before serving.
10. Cut the omelet into 2 portions and serve hot.

Turkey & Zucchini Omelet

Servings: 6
Preparation Time: 15 minutes
Cooking Time: 35 minutes

Ingredients:

- 8 eggs
- ½ cup unsweetened almond milk
- 1/8 teaspoon red pepper flakes, crushed
- Salt and ground black pepper, as required
- 1 cup cooked turkey meat, chopped
- 1 cup Monterrey Jack cheese, shredded
- ½ cup fresh scallion, chopped
- ¾ cup zucchini, chopped

Instructions:

1. In a bowl, add the eggs, almond milk, salt and black pepper and beat well.
2. Add the remaining ingredients and stir to combine.
3. Place the mixture into a greased baking dish.
4. Select "Bake" of Breville Smart Air Fryer Oven and adjust the temperature to 315 degrees F.
5. Set the timer for 35 minutes and press "Start/Stop" to begin preheating.
6. When the unit beeps to show that it is preheated, arrange the baking dish over the wire rack.
7. When the cooking time is complete, remove the baking dish from the oven and place onto a wire rack to cool for about 5 minutes before serving.
8. Cut into equal-sized wedges and serve.

Pepperoni Omelet

Servings: 2
Preparation Time: 15 minutes
Cooking Time: 12 minutes

Ingredients:

- 4 eggs
- 2 tablespoons milk
- Pinch of salt
- Ground black pepper, as required
- 8-10 turkey pepperoni slices

Instructions:

1. In a bowl, crack the eggs and beat well.
2. Add the remaining ingredients and gently stir to combine.
3. Place the mixture into a baking dish.
4. Select "Air Fry" of Breville Smart Air Fryer Oven and adjust the temperature to 355 degrees F.
5. Set the timer for 12 minutes and press "Start/Stop" to begin preheating.
6. When the unit beeps to show that it is preheated, arrange the baking dish over the wire rack.
7. When the cooking time is complete, remove the baking dish from oven.
8. Cut into equal-sized wedges and serve.

Egg & Tofu Omelet

Servings: 2
Preparation Time: 15 minutes
Cooking Time: 10 minutes

Ingredients:

- 1 teaspoon arrowroot starch
- 2 teaspoons water
- 3 eggs
- 2 teaspoons fish sauce
- 1 teaspoon olive oil
- Ground black pepper, as required
- 8 ounces silken tofu, pressed and sliced

Instructions:

1. In a large bowl, dissolve arrowroot starch in water.
2. Add the eggs, fish sauce, oil and black pepper and beat well.
3. Place tofu in the bottom of a greased baking dish and top with the egg mixture.
4. Select "Air Fry" of Breville Smart Air Fryer Oven and adjust the temperature to 390 degrees F.
5. Set the timer for 10 minutes and press "Start/Stop" to begin preheating.
6. When the unit beeps to show that it is preheated, arrange the baking dish over the wire rack.
7. When the cooking time is complete, remove the baking dish from oven and place onto a wire rack to cool for about 5 minutes before serving.
8. Cut into equal-sized wedges and serve.

Mini Veggie Frittatas

Servings: 2
Preparation Time: 15 minutes
Cooking Time: 17 minutes

Ingredients:

- 1 tablespoon butter
- ½ of white onion, sliced thinly
- 1 cup fresh mushrooms, sliced thinly
- 1¼ cups fresh spinach, chopped
- 3 eggs
- ½ teaspoon fresh rosemary, chopped
- Salt and ground black pepper, as required
- 3 tablespoons Parmesan cheese, shredded

Instructions:

1. In a frying pan, melt butter over medium heat and cook the onion and mushroom for about 3 minutes.
2. Add the spinach and cook for about 2-3 minutes.
3. Remove the frying pan from heat and set aside to cool slightly.
4. Meanwhile, in a small bowl, add the eggs, rosemary, salt and black pepper and beat well.
5. Divide the beaten eggs in 2 greased ramekins evenly and top with the veggie mixture, followed by the cheese.
6. Select "Air Fry" of Breville Smart Air Fryer Oven and adjust the temperature to 330 degrees F.
7. Set the timer for 12 minutes and press "Start/Stop" to begin preheating.
8. When the unit beeps to show that it is preheated, place the ramekins over the air rack.
9. When the cooking time is complete, remove the ramekins from the oven and place onto a wire rack for about 5 minutes before serving.

Spinach & Tomato Frittata

Servings: 6
Preparation Time: 15 minutes
Cooking Time: 30 minutes

Ingredients:

- 10 large eggs

- Salt and ground black pepper, as required
- 1 (5-ounce) bag baby spinach
- 2 cups grape tomatoes, halved
- 4 scallions, sliced thinly
- 8 ounces feta cheese, crumbled
- 3 tablespoons hot olive oil

Instructions:

1. In a bowl, place the eggs, salt and black pepper and beat well.
2. Add the spinach, tomatoes, scallions and feta cheese and gently stir to combine.
3. Spread the oil in a baking dish and top with the spinach mixture.
4. Select "Bake" of Breville Smart Air Fryer Oven and adjust the temperature to 350 degrees F.
5. Set the timer for 30 minutes and press "Start/Stop" to begin preheating.
6. When the unit beeps to show that it is preheated, arrange the baking dish over the wire rack.
7. When the cooking time is complete, remove the baking dish from oven and place onto a wire rack to cool for about 5 minutes before serving.
8. Cut into equal-sized wedges and serve.

Beef Frittata

Servings: 4
Preparation Time: 15 minutes
Cooking Time: 20 minutes

Ingredients:

- ½ pound cooked ground beef, grease removed
- 1 cup Colby Jack cheese, shredded
- 8 eggs, beaten lightly
- 4 scallions, chopped
- 1/8 teaspoon red pepper flakes, crushed
- Salt and ground black pepper, as required

Instructions:

1. In a bowl, add the sausage, cheese, eggs, scallion and cayenne and mix until well combined.
2. Place the mixture into a greased baking dish.
3. Select "Air Fry" of Breville Smart Air Fryer Oven and adjust the temperature to 360 degrees F.
4. Set the timer for 20 minutes and press "Start/Stop" to begin preheating.

5. When the unit beeps to show that it is preheated, arrange the baking dish over the wire rack.
6. When the cooking time is complete, remove the baking dish from oven and place onto a wire rack to cool for about 5 minutes before serving.
7. Cut into 4 wedges and serve.

Trout Frittata

Servings: 4
Preparation Time: 15 minutes
Cooking Time: 25 minutes

Ingredients:

- 1 tablespoon olive oil
- 1 onion, sliced
- 6 eggs
- ½ tablespoon horseradish sauce
- 2 tablespoons crème fraiche
- 2 hot-smoked trout fillets, chopped
- ¼ cup fresh dill, chopped

Instructions:

1. In a skillet, heat the oil over medium heat and cook the onion for about 4–5 minutes.
2. Remove from the heat and set aside.
3. Meanwhile, in a bowl, add the eggs, horseradish sauce, and crème fraiche and mix well.
4. In the bottom of a baking dish, place the cooked onion and top with the egg mixture, followed by trout.
5. Select "Air Fry" of Breville Smart Air Fryer Oven and adjust the temperature to 320 degrees F.
6. Set the timer for 20 minutes and press "Start/Stop" to begin preheating.
7. When the unit beeps to show that it is preheated, arrange the baking dish over the wire rack.
8. When the cooking time is complete, remove the baking dish from oven and place onto a wire rack to cool for about 5 minutes before serving.
9. Cut into equal-sized wedges and serve with the garnishing of dill.

Tomato Quiche

Servings: 2
Preparation Time: 15 minutes
Cooking Time: 30 minutes

Ingredients:

- 4 eggs
- ¼ cup onion, chopped
- ½ cup tomatoes, chopped
- ½ cup milk
- 1 cup Gouda cheese, shredded
- Salt, as required

Instructions:

1. In a small baking dish, add all the ingredients and mix well.
2. Select "Air Fry" of Breville Smart Air Fryer Oven and adjust the temperature to 340 degrees F.
3. Set the timer for 30 minutes and press "Start/Stop" to begin preheating.
4. When the unit beeps to show that it is preheated, arrange the baking dish over the wire rack.
5. When the cooking time is complete, remove the baking dish from oven and place onto a wire rack to cool for about 5 minutes before serving.
6. Cut into equal-sized wedges and serve.

Chicken & Broccoli Quiche

Servings: 2
Preparation Time: 15 minutes
Cooking Time: 12 minutes

Ingredients:

- ½ of frozen ready-made pie crust
- ¼ tablespoon olive oil
- 1 small egg
- 3 tablespoons cheddar cheese, grated
- 1½ tablespoons whipping cream
- Salt and freshly ground black pepper, as needed
- 3 tablespoons boiled broccoli, chopped
- 2 tablespoons cooked chicken, chopped

Instructions:

1. Cut 1 (5-inch) round from the pie crust.
2. Arrange the pie crust round in a small pie pan and gently press in the bottom and sides.
3. In a bowl, mix together the egg, cheese, cream, salt, and black pepper.
4. Pour the egg mixture over the dough base and top with the broccoli and chicken.
5. Select "Air Fry" of Breville Smart Air Fryer Oven and adjust the temperature to 390 degrees F.
6. Set the timer for 12 minutes and press "Start/Stop" to begin preheating.
7. When the unit beeps to show that it is preheated, arrange the pie pan over the wire rack.
8. When the cooking time is complete, remove the pie pan from oven and place onto a wire rack to cool for about 5 minutes before serving.
9. Cut into equal-sized wedges and serve.

Bacon & Spinach Quiche

Servings: 4
Preparation Time: 15 minutes
Cooking Time: 12 minutes

Ingredients:

- 2 cooked bacon slices, chopped
- ½ cup fresh spinach, chopped
- ¼ cup mozzarella cheese, shredded
- ½ cup Parmesan cheese, shredded
- 2 tablespoons milk
- 2 dashes Tabasco sauce
- Salt and ground black pepper, as required

Instructions:

1. In a bowl, add all ingredients and mix well.
2. Transfer the mixture into a baking dish.
3. Select "Air Fry" of Breville Smart Air Fryer Oven and adjust the temperature to 320 degrees F.
4. Set the timer for 12 minutes and press "Start/Stop" to begin preheating.
5. When the unit beeps to show that it is preheated, arrange the baking dish over the wire rack.
6. When the cooking time is complete, remove the baking dish from oven and place onto a wire rack to cool for about 5 minutes before serving.
7. Cut into equal-sized wedges and serve hot.

Salmon Quiche

Servings: 2
Preparation Time: 15 minutes
Cooking Time: 20 minutes

Ingredients:

- 5½ ounces salmon fillet, chopped
- Salt and ground black pepper, as required
- ½ tablespoon fresh lemon juice
- 1 egg yolk
- 3½ tablespoons chilled butter
- 2/3 cup flour
- 1 tablespoon cold water
- 2 eggs
- 3 tablespoons whipping cream
- 1 scallion, chopped

Instructions:

1. In a bowl, add the salmon, salt, black pepper and lemon juice and mix well.
2. In another bowl, add the egg yolk, butter, flour and water and mix until a dough forms.
3. Place the dough onto a floured smooth surface and roll into about 7-inch round.
4. Place the dough in a quiche pan and press firmly in the bottom and along the edges.
5. Trim the excess edges.
6. In a small bowl, add the eggs, cream, salt and black pepper and beat until well combined.
7. Place the cream mixture over the crust evenly and top with the salmon mixture, followed by the scallion.
8. Select "Air Fry" of Breville Smart Air Fryer Oven and adjust the temperature to 355 degrees F.
9. Set the timer for 20 minutes and press "Start/Stop" to begin preheating.
10. When the unit beeps to show that it is preheated, arrange the quiche pan over the wire rack.
11. When the cooking time is complete, remove the quiche pan from the oven and set aside for about 5 minutes before serving.
12. Cut the quiche into equal-sized wedges and serve

Sausage & Mushroom Casserole

Servings: 6
Preparation Time: 15 minutes
Cooking Time: 19 minutes

Ingredients:

- 1 tablespoon olive oil
- ½ pound spicy ground sausage
- ¾ cup yellow onion, chopped
- 5 fresh mushrooms, sliced
- 8 eggs, beaten
- ½ teaspoon garlic salt
- ¾ cup Cheddar cheese, shredded and divided
- ¼ cup Alfredo sauce

Instructions:

1. In a skillet, heat the oil over medium heat and cook the sausage and onions for about 4-5 minutes.
2. Add the mushrooms and cook for about 6-7 minutes.
3. Remove from the oven and drain the grease from the skillet.
4. In a bowl, add the sausage mixture, beaten eggs, garlic salt, ½ cup of cheese and Alfredo sauce and stir to combine.
5. Place the sausage mixture into a baking dish.
6. Select "Air Fry" of Breville Smart Air Fryer Oven and adjust the temperature to 390 degrees F.
7. Set the timer for 12 minutes and press "Start/Stop" to begin preheating.
8. When the unit beeps to show that it is preheated, arrange the baking dish over the wire rack.
9. After 6 minutes of cooking, stir the sausage mixture well.
10. When the cooking time is complete, remove the baking dish from oven and place onto a wire rack to cool for about 5 minutes before serving.
11. Cut into equal-sized wedges and serve with the topping of remaining cheese.

Ham & Hashbrown Casserole

Servings: 5
Preparation Time: 15 minutes
Cooking Time: 35 minutes

Ingredients:

- 1½ tablespoons olive oil
- ½ of large onion, chopped
- 24 ounces frozen Hashbrown
- 3 eggs
- 2 tablespoons milk
- Salt and ground black pepper, as required
- ½ pound ham, chopped
- ¼ cup Cheddar cheese, shredded

Instructions:

1. In a skillet, heat the oil over medium heat and sauté the onion for about 4-5 minutes.
2. Remove from the heat and transfer the onion into a bowl.
3. Add the hashbrowns and mix well.
4. Place the mixture into a baking dish.
5. Select "Bake" of Breville Smart Air Fryer Oven and adjust the temperature to 350 degrees F.
6. Set the timer for 32 minutes and press "Start/Stop" to begin preheating.
7. When the unit beeps to show that it is preheated, arrange the baking dish over the wire rack.
8. Stir the mixture once after 8 minutes.
9. Meanwhile, in a bowl, add the eggs, milk, salt and black pepper and beat well.
10. After 15 minutes of cooking, place the egg mixture over hashbrown mixture evenly and top with the ham.
11. After 30 minutes of cooking, sprinkle the casserole with the cheese.
12. When the cooking time is complete, remove the baking dish from oven and place onto a wire rack to cool for about 5 minutes before serving.
13. Cut into equal-sized wedges and serve.

Eggs with Turkey & Spinach

Servings: 4
Preparation Time: 15 minutes
Cooking Time: 23 minutes

Ingredients:

- 1 tablespoon unsalted butter
- 1-pound fresh baby spinach
- 4 eggs
- 7 ounces cooked turkey, chopped
- 4 teaspoons milk
- Salt and ground black pepper, as required

Instructions:

1. In a skillet, melt the butter over medium heat and cook the spinach for about 2-3 minutes or until just wilted.
2. Remove from the heat and transfer the spinach into a bowl.
3. Set aside to cool slightly.
4. Divide the spinach into 4 greased ramekins, followed by the turkey.
5. Crack 1 egg into each ramekin and drizzle with milk.
6. Sprinkle with salt and black pepper.
7. Select "Air Fry" of Breville Smart Air Fryer Oven and adjust the temperature to 355 degrees F.
8. Set the timer for 20 minutes and press "Start/Stop" to begin preheating.
9. When the unit beeps to show that it is preheated, arrange the ramekins over the wire rack.
10. When the cooking time is complete, remove the ramekins from oven and place onto a wire rack to cool for about 5 minutes before serving.

Eggs with Ham

Servings: 2
Preparation Time: 10 minutes
Cooking Time: 13 minutes

Ingredients:

- 2 teaspoons unsalted butter, softened
- 2 ounces ham, sliced thinly
- 4 large eggs, divided
- Salt and ground black pepper, as required
- 2 tablespoons heavy cream
- 1/8 teaspoon smoked paprika
- 3 tablespoons Parmesan cheese, grated finely
- 2 teaspoons fresh chives, minced

Instructions:

1. In the bottom of a baking dish, spread the butter.
2. Arrange the ham slices over the butter.
3. In a bowl, add 1egg, salt, black pepper and cream and beat until smooth.
4. Place the egg mixture over the ham slices evenly.
5. Carefully crack the remaining eggs on top and sprinkle with paprika, salt, black pepper, cheese and chives evenly.
6. Select "Air Fry" of Breville Smart Air Fryer Oven and adjust the temperature to 320 degrees F.
7. Set the timer for 13 minutes and press "Start/Stop" to begin preheating.
8. When the unit beeps to show that it is preheated, arrange the baking dish over the wire rack.
9. When the cooking time is complete, remove the baking dish from the oven and set aside for about 5 minutes before serving.
10. Cut into equal-sized wedges and serve.

Cranberry Muffins

Servings: 8
Preparation Time: 25 minutes
Cooking Time: 15 minutes

Ingredients:

- ¼ cup unsweetened almond milk
- 2 large eggs
- ½ teaspoon vanilla extract
- 1½ cups almond flour
- ¼ cup Erythritol
- 1 teaspoon baking powder
- ¼ teaspoon ground cinnamon
- 1/8 teaspoon salt
- ½ cup fresh cranberries
- ¼ cup walnuts, chopped

Instructions:

1. In a blender, add the almond milk, eggs and vanilla extract and pulse for about 20-30 seconds.
2. Add the almond flour, Erythritol, baking powder, cinnamon and salt and pulse for about 30-45 seconds until well blended.
3. Transfer the mixture into a bowl.
4. Gently fold in half of the cranberries and walnuts.

5. Place the mixture into 8 silicone muffin cups and top each with remaining cranberries.
6. Select "Air Fry" of Breville Smart Air Fryer Oven and adjust the temperature to 325 degrees F.
7. Set the timer for 15 minutes and press "Start/Stop" to begin preheating.
8. When the unit beeps to show that it is preheated, arrange the muffin cups over the wire rack.
9. When the cooking time is complete, remove the muffin cups from oven and place onto a wire rack to cool for about 10 minutes.
10. Carefully invert the muffins onto the wire rack to completely cool before serving.

Blueberry Muffins

Servings: 12
Preparation Time: 16 minutes
Cooking Time: 12 minutes

Ingredients:

- 2 cups plus 2 tablespoons self-rising flour
- 5 tablespoons white sugar
- ½ cup milk
- 2 ounces butter, melted
- 2 eggs
- 2 teaspoons fresh orange zest, finely grated
- 2 tablespoons fresh orange juice
- ½ teaspoon vanilla extract
- ½ cup fresh blueberries

Instructions:

1. Grease 12 cups of the muffin tin. Set aside.
2. In a bowl, mix together the flour and white sugar.
3. In another large bowl, mix well the remaining ingredients except for blueberries.
4. Add the flour mixture and mix until just combined.
5. Fold in the blueberries.
6. Place the mixture into the prepared muffin cups.
7. Select "Air Fry" of Breville Smart Air Fryer Oven and adjust the temperature to 355 degrees F.
8. Set the timer for 12 minutes and press "Start/Stop" to begin preheating.
9. When the unit beeps to show that it is preheated, arrange the muffin tin over the wire rack.
10. When the cooking time is complete, remove the muffin tin from oven and place onto a wire rack to cool for about 10 minutes.

11. Carefully invert the muffins onto the wire rack to completely cool before serving.

Savory Carrot Muffins

Servings: 6
Preparation Time: 15 minutes
Cooking Time: 7 minutes

Ingredients:

For Muffins:

- ¼ cup whole-wheat flour
- ¼ cup all-purpose flour
- ½ teaspoon baking powder
- 1/8 teaspoon baking soda
- ½ teaspoon dried parsley, crushed
- ½ teaspoon salt
- ½ cup plain yogurt
- 1 teaspoon vinegar
- 1 tablespoon vegetable oil
- 3 tablespoons cottage cheese, grated
- 1 carrot, peeled and grated
- 2-4 tablespoons water (if needed)

For Topping:

- 7 ounces Parmesan cheese, grated
- ¼ cup walnuts, chopped

Instructions:

1. For muffins: in a large bowl, mix together the flours, baking powder, baking soda, parsley, and salt.
2. In another large bowl, add the yogurt and vinegar and mix well.
3. Add the remaining ingredients except for water and beat them well. (Add some water if needed).
4. Make a well in the center of the yogurt mixture.
5. Slowly add the flour mixture in the well and mix until well combined.
6. Place the mixture into lightly greased 6 medium-sized muffin molds evenly and top with the Parmesan cheese and walnuts.
7. Select "Air Fry" of Breville Smart Air Fryer Oven and adjust the temperature to 355 degrees F.

8. Set the timer for 7 minutes and press "Start/Stop" to begin preheating.
9. When the unit beeps to show that it is preheated, arrange the muffin molds over the wire rack.
10. When the cooking time is complete, remove the muffin molds from the oven and place onto a wire rack to cool for about 5 minutes.
11. Carefully invert the muffins onto the platter and serve warm.

Bacon & Spinach Muffins

Servings: 6
Preparation Time: 10 minutes
Cooking Time: 17 minutes

Ingredients:

- 6 eggs
- ½ cup milk
- Salt and ground black pepper, as required
- 1 cup fresh spinach, chopped
- 4 cooked bacon slices, crumbled

Instructions:

1. In a bowl, add the eggs, milk, salt and black pepper and beat until well combined.
2. Add the spinach and stir to combine.
3. Divide the spinach mixture into 6 greased cups of an egg bite mold evenly.
4. Select "Air Fry" of Breville Smart Air Fryer Oven and adjust the temperature to 325 degrees F.
5. Set the timer for 17 minutes and press "Start/Stop" to begin preheating.
6. When the unit beeps to show that it is preheated, arrange the egg bite mold over the wire rack.
7. When the cooking time is complete, remove the egg bite mold from oven and place onto a wire rack to cool for about 5 minutes.
8. Top with bacon pieces and serve warm.

Ham Muffins

Servings: 6
Preparation Time: q0 minutes
Cooking Time: 18 minutes

Ingredients:

- 6 ham slices
- 6 eggs
- 6 tablespoons cream
- 3 tablespoon mozzarella cheese, shredded
- ¼ teaspoon dried basil, crushed

Instructions:

1. Lightly grease 6 cups of the muffin tin.
2. Line each prepared muffin cup with 1 ham slice.
3. Crack 1 egg into each muffin cup and top with cream.
4. Sprinkle with cheese and basil.
5. Select "Air Fry" of Breville Smart Air Fryer Oven and adjust the temperature to 350 degrees F.
6. Set the timer for 18 minutes and press "Start/Stop" to begin preheating.
7. When the unit beeps to show that it is preheated, arrange the muffin tin over the wire rack.
8. When the cooking time is complete, remove the muffin tin from oven and place onto a wire rack to cool for about 10 minutes.
9. Carefully invert the muffins onto the platter and serve warm.

Yogurt Bread

Servings: 10
Preparation Time: 20 minutes
Cooking Time: 40 minutes

Ingredients:

- 1½ cups warm water, divided
- 1½ teaspoons active dry yeast
- 1 teaspoon sugar
- 3 cups all-purpose flour
- 1 cup plain Greek yogurt
- 2 teaspoons koasher salt

Instructions:

1. In the bowl of a stand mixer, fitted with the dough hook attachment, add ½ cup of the warm water, yeast and sugar and mix well.
2. Set aside for about 5 minutes.
3. Add the flour, yogurt, and salt and mix on medium-low speed until the dough comes together.
4. Then, mix on medium speed for 5 minutes.

5. Place the dough into a bowl.
6. With a plastic wrap, cover the bowl and place in a warm place for about 2-3 hours or until doubled in size.
7. Transfer the dough onto a lightly floured surface and shape into a smooth ball.
8. Place the dough onto a greased parchment paper-lined rack.
9. With a kitchen towel, cover the dough and let rest for 15 minutes.
10. With a very sharp knife, cut a 4x½-inch deep cut down the center of the dough.
11. Select "Roast" of Breville Smart Air Fryer Oven and adjust the temperature to 325 degrees F.
12. Set the timer for 40 minutes and press "Start/Stop" to begin preheating.
13. When the unit beeps to show that it is preheated, arrange the dough over the wire rack.
14. When the cooking time is complete, remove the bread from the oven and place onto a wire rack to cool completely before slicing.
15. Cut the bread into desired-sized slices and serve.

Date Bread

Servings: 10
Preparation Time: 15 minutes
Cooking Time: 22 minutes

Ingredients:

- 2½ cup dates, pitted and chopped
- ¼ cup butter
- 1 cup hot water
- 1½ cups flour
- ½ cup brown sugar
- 1 teaspoon baking powder
- 1 teaspoon baking soda
- ½ teaspoon salt
- 1 egg

Instructions:

1. In a large bowl, add the dates, butter and top with the hot water. Set aside for about 5 minutes.
2. In another bowl, mix together the flour, brown sugar, baking powder, baking soda, and salt.
3. In the same bowl of dates, add the flour mixture and egg and mix well.
4. Grease a baking dish.
5. Place the mixture into the prepared baking dish.

6. Select "Air Fry" of Breville Smart Air Fryer Oven and adjust the temperature to 340 degrees F.
7. Set the timer for 22 minutes and press "Start/Stop" to begin preheating.
8. When the unit beeps to show that it is preheated, arrange the baking dish over the wire rack.
9. When the cooking time is complete, remove the baking dish from oven and place onto a wire rack to cool for about 10 minutes.
10. Carefully invert the bread onto the wire rack to cool completely before slicing.
11. Cut the bread into desired-sized slices and serve.

Banana & Walnut Bread

Servings: 10
Preparation Time: 15 minutes
Cooking Time: 25 minutes

Ingredients:

- 1½ cups self-rising flour
- ¼ teaspoon bicarbonate of soda
- 5 tablespoons plus 1 teaspoon butter
- 2/3 cup plus ½ tablespoon caster sugar
- 2 medium eggs
- 3½ ounces walnuts, chopped
- 2 cups bananas, peeled and mashed

Instructions:

1. In a bowl, mix together the flour and bicarbonate of soda.
2. In another bowl, add the butter and sugar and beat until pale and fluffy.
3. Add the eggs, one at a time along with a little flour and mix well.
4. Stir in the remaining flour and walnuts.
5. Add the bananas and mix until well combined.
6. Grease a loaf pan.
7. Place the mixture into the prepared pan.
8. Select "Air Fry" of Breville Smart Air Fryer Oven and adjust the temperature to 355 degrees F.
9. Set the timer for 10 minutes and press "Start/Stop" to begin preheating.
10. When the unit beeps to show that it is preheated, arrange the loaf pan over the wire rack.
11. After 10 minutes of cooking, set the temperature at 338 degrees F for 15 minutes.

12. When the cooking time is complete, remove the loaf pan from oven and place onto a wire rack to cool for about 10 minutes.
13. Carefully invert the bread onto the wire rack to cool completely before slicing.
14. Cut the bread into desired-sized slices and serve.

Zucchini & Apple Bread

Servings: 8
Preparation Time: 15 minutes
Cooking Time: 30 minutes

Ingredients:

For Bread:

- 1 cup all-purpose flour
- ¾ teaspoon baking powder
- ¼ teaspoon baking soda
- 1¼ teaspoons ground cinnamon
- ¼ teaspoon salt
- 1/3 cup vegetable oil
- 1/3 cup sugar
- 1 egg
- 1 teaspoon vanilla extract
- ½ cup zucchini, shredded
- ½ cup apple, cored and shredded
- 5 tablespoons walnuts, chopped

For Topping:

- 1 tablespoon walnuts, chopped
- 2 teaspoons brown sugar
- ¼ teaspoon ground cinnamon

Instructions:

1. For bread: in a bowl, mix together the flour, baking powder, baking soda, cinnamon, and salt.
2. In another large bowl, mix well the oil, sugar, egg, and vanilla extract.
3. Add the flour mixture and mix until just combined.
4. Gently fold in the zucchini, apple and walnuts.
5. For the topping: in a small bowl, add all the ingredients and whisk them well.
6. Place the mixture into a lightly greased loaf pan and sprinkle with the topping mixture.

7. Select "Air Fry" of Breville Smart Air Fryer Oven and adjust the temperature to 325 degrees F.
8. Set the timer for 30 minutes and press "Start/Stop" to begin preheating.
9. When the unit beeps to show that it is preheated, arrange the loaf pan over the wire rack.
10. When the cooking time is complete, remove the loaf pan from oven and place the pan onto a wire rack to cool for about 10 minutes.
11. Carefully invert the bread onto the wire rack to cool completely before slicing.
12. Cut the bread into desired-sized slices and serve.

Carrot Bread

Servings: 6
Preparation Time: 15 minutes
Cooking Time: 30 minutes

Ingredients:

- 1 cup all-purpose flour
- 1 teaspoon baking soda
- ½ teaspoon ground cinnamon
- ¼ teaspoon ground cloves
- ¼ teaspoon ground nutmeg
- ½ teaspoon salt
- 2 large eggs
- ¾ cup vegetable oil
- 1/3 cup white sugar
- 1/3 cup light brown sugar
- ½ teaspoon vanilla extract
- 1½ cups carrots, peeled and grated

Instructions:

1. In a bowl, mix together the flour, baking soda, spices and salt.
2. In a large bowl, add the eggs, oil, sugars and vanilla extract and beat until well combined.
3. Add the flour mixture and mix until just combined.
4. Fold in the carrots.
5. Place the mixture into a lightly greased baking dish.
6. Select "Air Fry" of Breville Smart Air Fryer Oven and adjust the temperature to 320 degrees F.
7. Set the timer for 30 minutes and press "Start/Stop" to begin preheating.

8. When the unit beeps to show that it is preheated, arrange the baking dish over the wire rack and place onto a wire rack to cool for about 10 minutes.
9. Carefully invert the bread onto the wire rack to cool completely before slicing.
10. Cut the bread into desired-sized slices and serve.

Zucchini Fritters

Servings: 4
Preparation Time: 15 minutes
Cooking Time: 7 minutes

Ingredients:

- 10½ ounces zucchini, grated and squeezed
- 7 ounces Halloumi cheese
- ¼ cup all-purpose flour
- 2 eggs
- 1 teaspoon fresh dill, minced
- Salt and ground black pepper, as required

Instructions:

1. In a large bowl and mix together all the ingredients.
2. Make small-sized fritters from the mixture.
3. Arrange the fritters into the greased enamel roasting pan.
4. Select "Air Fry" of Breville Smart Air Fryer Oven and adjust the temperature to 355 degrees F.
5. Set the timer for 7 minutes and press "Start/Stop" to begin preheating.
6. When the unit beeps to show that it is preheated, insert the roasting pan in the oven.
7. When the cooking time is complete, remove the roasting pan from the oven.
8. Serve warm.

Pumpkin Pancakes

Servings: 4
Preparation Time: 15 minutes
Cooking Time: 12 minutes

Ingredients:

- 1 square puff pastry

- 3 tablespoons pumpkin filling
- 1 small egg, beaten

Instructions:

1. Roll out a puff pastry square and layer it with pumpkin pie filling, leaving about ¼-inch space around the edges.
2. Cut it up into 8 equal-sized square pieces and coat the edges with beaten egg.
3. Arrange the squares into the greased enamel roasting pan.
4. Select "Air Fry" of Breville Smart Air Fryer Oven and adjust the temperature to 355 degrees F.
5. Set the timer for 12 minutes and press "Start/Stop" to begin preheating.
6. When the unit beeps to show that it is preheated, insert the roasting pan in the oven.
7. When the cooking time is complete, remove the roasting pan from the oven.
8. Serve warm.

Snacks & Side Dishes Recipes

Roasted Cashews

Servings: 6
Preparation Time: 5 minutes
Cooking Time: 5 minutes

Ingredients:

- 1½ cups raw cashew nuts
- 1 teaspoon butter, melted
- Salt and freshly ground black pepper, as required

Instructions:

1. In a bowl, mix together all the ingredients.
2. Arrange the cashews into the air fry basket.
3. Select "Air Fry" of Breville Smart Air Fryer Oven and adjust the temperature to 355 degrees F.
4. Set the timer for 5 minutes and press "Start/Stop" to begin preheating.
5. When the unit beeps to show that it is preheated, insert the air fry basket in the oven.
6. Shake the cashews once halfway through.
7. When the cooking time is complete, remove the air fry basket from the oven and set aside to cool completely before serving.

Spicy Chickpeas

Servings: 4
Preparation Time: 5 minutes
Cooking Time: 10 minutes

Ingredients:

- 1 (15-ounce) can chickpeas, rinsed and drained
- 1 tablespoon olive oil
- ½ teaspoon ground cumin
- ½ teaspoon cayenne pepper
- ½ teaspoon smoked paprika
- Salt, as required

Instructions:

1. In a bowl, add all the ingredients and toss to coat well.
2. Arrange the chickpeas into the air fry basket.
3. Select "Air Fry" of Breville Smart Air Fryer Oven and adjust the temperature to 390 degrees F.
4. Set the timer for 10 minutes and press "Start/Stop" to begin preheating.
5. When the unit beeps to show that it is preheated, insert the air fry basket in the oven.
6. When the cooking time is complete, remove the air fry basket from the oven and set aside to cool completely before serving.

Kale Chips

Servings: 4
Preparation Time: 10 minutes
Cooking Time: 7 minutes

Ingredients:

- 1 (8-ounce) bunch curly kale, tough ribs removed and torn into 2-inch pieces
- 1 tablespoon olive oil
- 1 teaspoon salt

Instructions:

1. In a large bowl, add all the ingredients and with your hands, massage the oil and salt into kale completely.
2. Arrange the kale pieces onto 2 wire racks.
3. Select "Air Fry" of Breville Smart Air Fryer Oven and adjust the temperature to 340 degrees F.
4. Set the timer for 7 minutes and press "Start/Stop" to begin preheating.
5. When the unit beeps to show that it is preheated, insert 1 rack in the top position and another in the bottom position.
6. Insert 1 tray in the top position and another in the bottom position.
7. Switch the position of enamel roasting pans once halfway through.
8. When the cooking time is complete, remove the wire racks from the oven and transfer the kale chips into a bowl.
9. Serve hot.

Apple Chips

Servings: 2
Preparation Time: 10 minutes
Cooking Time: 8 minutes

Ingredients:

- 1 apple, peeled, cored and thinly sliced
- 1 tablespoon sugar
- ½ teaspoon ground cinnamon
- Pinch of ground cardamom
- Pinch of ground ginger
- Pinch of salt

Instructions:

1. In a bowl, add all the ingredients and toss to coat well.
2. Arrange the apple chips into the air fry basket.
3. Select "Air Fry" of Breville Smart Air Fryer Oven and adjust the temperature to 390 degrees F.
4. Set the timer for 8 minutes and press "Start/Stop" to begin preheating.
5. When the unit beeps to show that it is preheated, insert the air fry basket in the oven.
6. When the cooking time is complete, remove the air fry basket from the oven and set aside to cool completely before serving.

French Fries

Servings: 4
Preparation Time: 15 minutes
Cooking Time: 30 minutes

Ingredients:

- 1-pound potatoes, peeled and cut into strips
- 3 tablespoons olive oil
- ½ teaspoon onion powder
- ½ teaspoon garlic powder
- 1 teaspoon paprika

Instructions:

1. In a large bowl of water, soak the potato strips for about 1 hour.

2. Drain the potato strips well and pat them dry with paper towels.
3. In a large bowl, add the potato strips and the remaining ingredients and toss to coat well.
4. Arrange the potato fries into the air fry basket.
5. Select "Air Fry" of Breville Smart Air Fryer Oven and adjust the temperature to 375 degrees F.
6. Set the timer for 30 minutes and press "Start/Stop" to begin preheating.
7. When the unit beeps to show that it is preheated, insert the air fry basket in the oven.
8. When the cooking time is complete, remove the air fry basket from the oven and set aside to cool slightly before serving.
9. Serve warm.

Tortilla Chips

Servings: 3
Preparation Time: 10 minutes
Cooking Time: 3 minutes

Ingredients:

- 4 corn tortillas, cut into triangles
- 1 tablespoon olive oil
- Salt, to taste

Instructions:

1. Coat the tortilla chips with oil and then sprinkle each side of the tortillas with salt.
2. Arrange the tortilla chips into the air fry basket.
3. Select "Air Fry" of Breville Smart Air Fryer Oven and adjust the temperature to 390 degrees F.
4. Set the timer for 3 minutes and press "Start/Stop" to begin preheating.
5. When the unit beeps to show that it is preheated, insert the air fry basket in the oven.
6. When the cooking time is complete, remove the air fry basket from the oven and set aside to cool slightly before serving.
7. Serve warm.

Crispy Eggplant Slices

Servings: 4
Preparation Time: 15 minutes
Cooking Time: 8 minutes

Ingredients:

- 1 medium eggplant, peeled and cut into ½-inch round slices
- Salt, as required
- ½ cup all-purpose flour
- 2 eggs, beaten
- 1 cup Italian-style breadcrumbs
- ¼ cup olive oil

Instructions:

1. In a colander, add the eggplant slices and sprinkle with salt. Set aside for about 45 minutes.
2. With paper towels, pat dry the eggplant slices.
3. In a shallow dish, place the flour.
4. Crack the eggs in a second dish and beat well.
5. In a third dish, mix together the oil and breadcrumbs.
6. Coat each eggplant slice with flour, then dip into beaten eggs and finally, coat with the breadcrumb's mixture.
7. Arrange the eggplant slices into the air fry basket.
8. Select "Air Fry" of Breville Smart Air Fryer Oven and adjust the temperature to 390 degrees F.
9. Set the timer for 8 minutes and press "Start/Stop" to begin preheating.
10. When the unit beeps to show that it is preheated, insert the air fry basket in the oven.
11. When the cooking time is complete, remove the air fry basket from the oven and set aside to cool slightly before serving.
12. Serve warm.

Cauliflower Popcorns

Servings: 4
Preparation Time: 15 minutes
Cooking Time: 12 hours

Ingredients:

- 1 (2-pound) head cauliflower, cut into small florets
- 2 tablespoons hot sauce
- 1 tablespoon fresh lime juice
- 1 tablespoon oil
- 1 tablespoon smoked paprika
- 1 teaspoon ground cumin

Instructions:

1. In a bowl, add all the ingredients and toss to coat well.
2. Arrange the cauliflower florets onto 2 wire racks.
3. Select "Dehydrate" of Breville Smart Air Fryer Oven and adjust the temperature to 130 degrees F.
4. Set the timer for 12 hours and press "Start/Stop" to begin preheating.
5. When the unit beeps to show that it is preheated, insert 1 rack in the top position and another in the bottom position.
6. Switch the position of wire racks once halfway through.
7. When the cooking time is complete, remove the wire racks from the oven and transfer the cauliflower florets into a bowl.
8. Serve hot.

Broccoli Poppers

Servings: 4
Preparation Time: 15 minutes
Cooking Time: 10 minutes

Ingredients:

- 2 tablespoons plain yogurt
- ½ teaspoon red chili powder
- ¼ teaspoon ground cumin
- ¼ teaspoon ground turmeric
- Salt, as required
- 1 pound broccoli, cut into small florets
- 2 tablespoons chickpea flour

Instructions:

1. In a bowl, mix together the yogurt and spices.
2. Add the broccoli and coat with marinade generously.
3. Refrigerate for about 20 minutes.
4. Arrange the broccoli florets into the air fry basket.
5. Select "Air Fry" of Breville Smart Air Fryer Oven and adjust the temperature to 400 degrees F.
6. Set the timer for 10 minutes and press "Start/Stop" to begin preheating.
7. When the unit beeps to show that it is preheated, insert the air fry basket in the oven.

8. When the cooking time is complete, remove the air fry basket from the oven and set aside to cool slightly before serving.
9. Serve warm.

Mozzarella Sticks

Servings: 3
Preparation Time: 15 minutes
Cooking Time: 12 minutes

Ingredients:

- ¼ cup white flour
- 2 eggs
- 3 tablespoons nonfat milk
- 1 cup plain breadcrumbs
- 1 pound Mozzarella cheese block cut into 3x½-inch sticks

Instructions:

1. In a shallow dish, add the flour.
2. In a second shallow dish, mix together the eggs, and milk.
3. In a third shallow dish, place the breadcrumbs.
4. Coat the Mozzarella sticks with flour, then dip into egg mixture and finally, coat with the breadcrumbs.
5. Arrange the mozzarella sticks into the air fry basket.
6. Select "Air Fry" of Breville Smart Air Fryer Oven and adjust the temperature to 400 degrees F.
7. Set the timer for 12 minutes and press "Start/Stop" to begin preheating.
8. When the unit beeps to show that it is preheated, insert the air fry basket in the oven.
9. When the cooking time is complete, remove the air fry basket from the oven and set aside to cool slightly before serving.
10. Serve warm.

Chicken Nuggets

Servings: 6
Preparation Time: 15 minutes
Cooking Time: 10 minutes

Ingredients:

- 2 large chicken breasts, cut into 1-inch cubes
- 1 cup breadcrumbs
- 1/3 tablespoon Parmesan cheese, shredded
- 1 teaspoon onion powder
- ¼ teaspoon smoked paprika
- Salt and ground black pepper, as required

Instructions:

1. In a large resealable bag, add all the ingredients.
2. Seal the bag and shake well to coat completely.
3. Arrange the nuggets into the greased air fry basket.
4. Select "Air Fry" of Breville Smart Air Fryer Oven and adjust the temperature to 400 degrees F.
5. Set the timer for 10 minutes and press "Start/Stop" to begin preheating.
6. When the unit beeps to show that it is preheated, insert the air fry basket in the oven.
7. When the cooking time is complete, remove the air fry basket from the oven and set aside to cool slightly before serving.

Bacon Croquettes

Servings: 8
Preparation Time: 15 minutes
Cooking Time: 8 minutes

Ingredients:

- 1-pound sharp cheddar cheese block
- 1-pound thin bacon slices
- 1 cup all-purpose flour
- 3 eggs
- 1 cup breadcrumbs
- Salt, as required
- ¼ cup olive oil

Instructions:

1. Cut the cheese block into 1-inch rectangular pieces.
2. Wrap 2 bacon slices around 1 piece of cheddar cheese, covering completely.
3. Repeat with the remaining bacon and cheese pieces.

4. Arrange the croquettes in a baking dish and freeze for about 5 minutes.
5. In a shallow dish, place the flour.
6. In a second dish, crack the eggs and beat well.
7. In a third dish, mix together the breadcrumbs, salt, and oil.
8. Coat the croquettes with flour, then dip into beaten eggs and finally, coat with the breadcrumbs mixture.
9. Arrange the croquettes into the greased air fry basket.
10. Select "Air Fry" of Breville Smart Air Fryer Oven and adjust the temperature to 390 degrees F.
11. Set the timer for 8 minutes and press "Start/Stop" to begin preheating.
12. When the unit beeps to show that it is preheated, insert the air fry basket in the oven.
13. When the cooking time is complete, remove the air fry basket from the oven and set aside to cool slightly before serving.

Buffalo Chicken Wings

Servings: 5
Preparation Time: 15 minutes
Cooking Time: 16 minutes

Ingredients:

- 2 pounds frozen chicken wings, drums and flats separated
- 2 tablespoons olive oil
- 2 tablespoons Buffalo sauce
- ½ teaspoon red pepper flakes, crushed
- Salt, as required

Instructions:

1. Coat the chicken wings with oil evenly.
2. Arrange the chicken wings into the greased air fry basket.
3. Select "Air Fry" of Breville Smart Air Fryer Oven and adjust the temperature to 390 degrees F.
4. Set the timer for 16 minutes and press "Start/Stop" to begin preheating.
5. When the unit beeps to show that it is preheated, insert the air fry basket in the oven.
6. After 7 minutes, flip the wings.
7. Meanwhile, in a large bowl, add the buffalo sauce, red pepper flakes and salt and mix well.

8. When the cooking time is complete, remove the air fry basket from the oven.
9. Transfer the wings into the bowl of Buffalo sauce and toss to coat well.
10. Serve immediately.

Crispy Prawns

Servings: 4
Preparation Time: 15 minutes
Cooking Time: 8 minutes

Ingredients:

- 1 egg
- ½ pound nacho chips, crushed
- 12 prawns, peeled and deveined

Instructions:

1. In a shallow dish, beat the egg.
2. In another shallow dish, place the crushed nacho chips.
3. Coat the prawn into the egg and then roll into nacho chips.
4. Arrange the prawns into the greased air fry basket.
5. Select "Air Fry" of Breville Smart Air Fryer Oven and adjust the temperature to 355 degrees F.
6. Set the timer for 8 minutes and press "Start/Stop" to begin preheating.
7. When the unit beeps to show that it is preheated, insert the air fry basket in the oven.
8. When the cooking time is complete, remove the air fry basket from the oven.
9. Serve immediately.

Bacon-Wrapped Shrimp

Servings: 6
Preparation Time: 15 minutes
Cooking Time: 7 minutes

Ingredients:

- 1 pound bacon, sliced thinly
- 1 pound shrimp, peeled and deveined

Instructions:

1. Wrap one slice of bacon around each shrimp completely.
2. Arrange the shrimp in a baking dish and refrigerate for about 20 minutes.
3. Arrange the shrimp into the greased air fry basket.
4. Select "Air Fry" of Breville Smart Air Fryer Oven and adjust the temperature to 390 degrees F.
5. Set the timer for 6 minutes and press "Start/Stop" to begin preheating.
6. When the unit beeps to show that it is preheated, insert the air fry basket in the oven.
7. When the cooking time is complete, remove the air fry basket from the oven.
8. Serve immediately.

Feta Tater Tots

Servings: 6
Preparation Time: 15 minutes
Cooking Time: 25 minutes

Ingredients:

- 2 pounds frozen tater tots
- ½ cup feta cheese, crumbled
- ½ cup tomato, chopped
- ¼ cup black olives, pitted and sliced
- ¼ cup red onion, chopped

Instructions:

1. Arrange the tater tots into the greased air fry basket.
2. Select "Air Fry" of Breville Smart Air Fryer Oven and adjust the temperature to 450 degrees F.
3. Set the timer for 15 minutes and press "Start/Stop" to begin preheating.
4. When the unit beeps to show that it is preheated, insert the air fry basket in the oven.
5. When the cooking time is complete, remove the air fry basket from the oven and transfer tots into a large bowl.
6. Add the feta cheese, tomatoes, olives and onion and toss to coat well.
7. Now, place the mixture into an enamel roasting pan.
8. Select "Air Fry" of Breville Smart Air Fryer Oven and adjust the temperature to 450 degrees F.

>8

Breville Smart Air Fryer Cookbook

9. Set the timer for 10 minutes and insert the roasting pan in the oven.
10. Press "Start/Stop" to begin cooking.
11. When the cooking time is complete, remove the roasting pan from the oven.
12. Serve warm.

Buttermilk Biscuits

Servings: 8
Preparation Time: 15 minutes
Cooking Time: 8 minutes

Ingredients:

- ½ cup cake flour
- 1¼ cups all-purpose flour
- ¼ teaspoon baking soda
- ½ teaspoon baking powder
- 1 teaspoon granulated sugar
- Salt, to taste
- ¼ cup cold unsalted butter, cut into cubes
- ¾ cup buttermilk
- 2 tablespoons butter, melted

Instructions:

1. In a large bowl, sift together flours, baking soda, baking powder, sugar and salt.
2. With a pastry cutter, cut cold butter and mix until coarse crumb forms.
3. Slowly add buttermilk and mix until a smooth dough forms.
4. Place the dough onto a floured surface and with your hands, press it into ½ inch thickness.
5. With a 1¾-inch round cookie cutter, cut the biscuits.
6. Arrange the biscuits into a baking dish in a single layer and coat with the butter.
7. Select "Air Fry" of Breville Smart Air Fryer Oven and adjust the temperature to 400 degrees F.
8. Set the timer for 18minutes and press "Start/Stop" to begin preheating.
9. When the unit beeps to show that it is preheated, arrange the baking dish over the wire rack.
10. When the cooking time is complete, remove the baking dish from the oven and place onto a wire rack for about 5 minutes.
11. Carefully invert the biscuits onto the wire rack to cool completely before serving.

Cheddar Biscuits

Servings: 8
Preparation Time: 15 minutes
Cooking Time: 10 minutes

Ingredients:

- 1/3 cup unbleached all-purpose flour
- 1/8 teaspoon cayenne pepper
- 1/8 teaspoon smoked paprika
- Pinch of garlic powder
- Salt and ground black pepper, as required
- ½ cup sharp cheddar cheese, shredded
- 2 tablespoons butter, softened
- Nonstick cooking spray

Instructions:

1. In a food processor, add the flour, spices, salt and black pepper and pulse until well combined.
2. Add the cheese and butter and pulse until a smooth dough forms.
3. Place the dough onto a lightly floured surface.
4. Make 16 small equal-sized balls from the dough and press each slightly.
5. Arrange the biscuits into the greased air fry basket.
6. Select "Bake" of Breville Smart Air Fryer Oven and adjust the temperature to 330 degrees F.
7. Set the timer for 10 minutes and press "Start/Stop" to begin preheating.
8. When the unit beeps to show that it is preheated, insert the air fry basket in the oven.
9. When the cooking time is complete, remove the air fry basket from the oven and place onto a wire rack for about 10 minutes.
10. Carefully invert the biscuits onto the wire rack to cool completely before serving.

Chili Dip

Servings: 8
Preparation Time: 10 minutes
Cooking Time: 15 minutes

Ingredients:

- 1 (8-ounce) package cream cheese, softened

- 1 (16-ounce) can Hormel chili without beans
- 1 (16-ounce) package mild cheddar cheese, shredded

Instructions:

1. In a baking dish, place the cream cheese and spread in an even layer.
2. Top with chili evenly, followed by the cheese.
3. Select "Bake" of Breville Smart Air Fryer Oven and adjust the temperature to 375 degrees F.
4. Set the timer for 15 minutes and press "Start/Stop" to begin preheating.
5. When the unit beeps to show that it is preheated, arrange the baking dish over the wire rack.
6. When the cooking time is complete, remove the baking dish from the oven.
7. Serve hot.

3-Cheeses Onion Dip

Servings: 10
Preparation Time: 10 minutes
Cooking Time: 45 minutes

Ingredients:

- 2/3 cup onion, chopped
- 1 cup cheddar jack cheese, shredded
- ½ cup Swiss cheese, shredded
- ¼ cup Parmesan cheese, shredded
- 2/3 cup whipped salad dressing
- ½ cup milk
- Salt, as required

Instructions:

1. In a large bowl, add all the ingredients and mix well.
2. Transfer the mixture into a baking dish and spread in an even layer.
3. Select "Bake" of Breville Smart Air Fryer Oven and adjust the temperature to 375 degrees F.
4. Set the timer for 45 minutes and press "Start/Stop" to begin preheating.
5. When the unit beeps to show that it is preheated, insert the baking dish in the oven.
6. When the cooking time is complete, remove the baking dish from the oven.
7. Serve hot.

Basil Tomatoes

Servings: 2
Preparation Time: 10 minutes
Cooking Time: 10 minutes

Ingredients:

- 3 tomatoes, halved
- Olive oil cooking spray
- Salt and ground black pepper, as required
- 1 tablespoon fresh basil, chopped

Instructions:

1. Drizzle the cut sides of the tomato halves with cooking spray evenly.
2. Sprinkle with salt, black pepper and basil.
3. Arrange the tomato halves into the air fry basket, cut side-up.
4. Select "Air Fry" of Breville Smart Air Fryer Oven and adjust the temperature to 320 degrees F.
5. Set the timer for 10 minutes and press "Start/Stop" to begin preheating.
6. When the unit beeps to show that it is preheated, insert the air fry basket in the oven.
7. When the cooking time is complete, remove the air fry basket from the oven.
8. Serve warm.

Pesto Tomatoes

Servings: 4
Preparation Time: 10 minutes
Cooking Time: 14 minutes

Ingredients:

- 3 large heirloom tomatoes, cut into ½ inch thick slices.
- 1 cup pesto
- 8 ounces feta cheese, cut into ½ inch thick slices
- ½ cup red onions, sliced thinly
- 1 tablespoon olive oil

Instructions:

1. Spread some pesto on each slice of tomato.

2. Top each tomato slice with a feta slice and onion and drizzle with oil.
3. Arrange the tomato slices into the air fry basket, cut side-up.
4. Select "Air Fry" of Breville Smart Air Fryer Oven and adjust the temperature to 390 degrees F.
5. Set the timer for 14 minutes and press "Start/Stop" to begin preheating.
6. When the unit beeps to show that it is preheated, insert the air fry basket in the oven.
7. When the cooking time is complete, remove the air fry basket from the oven.
8. Serve warm.

Herbed Bell Peppers

Servings: 4
Preparation Time: 10 minutes
Cooking Time: 8 minutes

Ingredients:

- 1½ pounds bell peppers, seeded and cubed
- ½ teaspoon dried thyme, crushed
- ½ teaspoon dried savory, crushed
- Salt and ground black pepper, as required
- 2 teaspoons butter, melted

Instructions:

1. In a bowl, add the bell peppers, herbs, salt and black pepper and toss to coat well.
2. Arrange the bell peppers into the greased air fry basket.
3. Select "Air Fry" of Breville Smart Air Fryer Oven and adjust the temperature to 360 degrees F.
4. Set the timer for 8 minutes and press "Start/Stop" to begin preheating.
5. When the unit beeps to show that it is preheated, insert the air fry basket in the oven.
6. When the cooking time is complete, remove the air fry basket from the oven and transfer the bell peppers into a bowl.
7. Drizzle with butter and serve immediately.

Balsamic Green Beans

Servings: 3
Preparation Time: 10 minutes
Cooking Time: 12 minutes

Ingredients:

- 1-pound green beans, trimmed
- 2 garlic cloves, minced
- 1 tablespoon vegetable oil
- 1 tablespoon balsamic vinegar
- Salt and ground black pepper, as required

Instructions:

1. In a large bowl, add all the ingredients and toss to coat well.
2. Arrange the green beans into the greased air fry basket in a single layer.
3. Select "Air Fry" of Breville Smart Air Fryer Oven and adjust the temperature to 400 degrees F.
4. Set the timer for 12 minutes and press "Start/Stop" to begin preheating.
5. When the unit beeps to show that it is preheated, insert the air fry basket in the oven.
6. When the cooking time is complete, remove the air fry basket from the oven.
7. Serve hot.

Buttered Asparagus

Servings: 3
Preparation Time: 10 minutes
Cooking Time: 6 minutes

Ingredients:

- 1 pound asparagus, trimmed
- 2 tablespoons butter, melted
- 2 tablespoons fresh lemon juice
- Salt and ground black pepper, as required

Instructions:

1. In a bowl, mix together the asparagus, butter, lemon juice, salt, and black pepper.
2. Arrange the asparagus into the greased air fry basket in a single layer.
3. Select "Air Fry" of Breville Smart Air Fryer Oven and adjust the temperature to 400 degrees F.
4. Set the timer for 6 minutes and press "Start/Stop" to begin preheating.
5. When the unit beeps to show that it is preheated, insert the air fry basket in the oven.

6. When the cooking time is complete, remove the air fry basket from the oven and transfer the asparagus into a bowl.
7. Serve hot.

Parmesan Broccoli

Servings: 6
Preparation Time: 15 minutes
Cooking Time: 15 minutes

Ingredients:

- 1½ pounds broccoli head, stemmed and cut into 1-inch florets
- 2 tablespoons olive oil
- Salt and ground black pepper, as required
- 2 teaspoons fresh lemon zest, grated
- ¼ cup Parmesan cheese, grated

Instructions:

1. In a pan of the boiling water, add the broccoli and cook for about 3-4 minutes.
2. Drain the broccoli well.
3. In a bowl, place the broccoli, oil, salt, and black pepper and toss to coat well.
4. Arrange the broccoli florets into the greased air fry basket in a single layer.
5. Select "Air Fry" of Breville Smart Air Fryer Oven and adjust the temperature to 355 degrees F.
6. Set the timer for 15 minutes and press "Start/Stop" to begin preheating.
7. When the unit beeps to show that it is preheated, insert the air fry basket in the oven.
8. After 8 minutes of cooking, toss the broccoli florets.
9. When the cooking time is complete, remove the air fry basket from the oven and transfer the broccoli florets into a bowl.
10. Immediately stir in the olives, lemon zest and cheese.
11. Serve immediately.

Curried Cauliflower

Servings: 4
Preparation Time: 15 minutes
Cooking Time: 10 minutes

Ingredients:

- 2 tablespoons golden raisins
- ½ head cauliflower, cored and cut into 1-inch pieces
- ½ cup olive oil, divided
- ½ tablespoon curry powder
- Salt, as required
- 2 tablespoons pine nuts, toasted

Instructions:

1. Soak the raisins in boiling water and set aside.
2. In a bowl, mix together the cauliflower, oil, curry powder and salt.
3. Arrange the cauliflower florets into the greased air fry basket in a single layer.
4. Select "Air Fry" of Breville Smart Air Fryer Oven and adjust the temperature to 390 degrees F.
5. Set the timer for 10 minutes and press "Start/Stop" to begin preheating.
6. When the unit beeps to show that it is preheated, insert the air fry basket in the oven.
7. When the cooking time is complete, remove the air fry basket from the oven and transfer the cauliflower florets into a bowl.
8. Drain the golden raisins into a strainer.
9. In the bowl of cauliflower, add the raisins and pine nuts and toss to coat.
10. Serve immediately.

Spicy Butternut Squash

Servings: 3
Preparation Time: 15 minutes
Cooking Time: 20 minutes

Ingredients:

- 1 medium butternut squash, peeled, seeded and cut into chunk
- 2 teaspoons cumin seeds
- 1/8 teaspoon garlic powder
- 1/8 teaspoon chili flakes, crushed
- Salt and ground black pepper, as required
- 1 tablespoon olive oil
- 2 tablespoons pine nuts
- 2 tablespoons fresh cilantro, chopped

Instructions:

1. In a bowl, mix together the squash, spices, and oil.
2. Arrange the squash chunks into the greased air fry basket.
3. Select "Air Fry" of Breville Smart Air Fryer Oven and adjust the temperature to 375 degrees F.
4. Set the timer for 20 minutes and press "Start/Stop" to begin preheating.
5. When the unit beeps to show that it is preheated, insert the air fry basket in the oven.
6. When the cooking time is complete, remove the air fry basket from the oven and transfer the squash chunks into a bowl.
7. Serve hot with the garnishing of pine nuts and cilantro.

Caramelized Baby Carrots

Servings: 4
Preparation Time: 10 minutes
Cooking Time: 15 minutes

Ingredients:

- ½ cup butter, melted
- ½ cup brown sugar
- 1 pound bag baby carrots

Instructions:

1. In a bowl, mix together the butter, brown sugar and carrots.
2. Arrange the carrots into the greased air fry basket.
3. Select "Air Fry" of Breville Smart Air Fryer Oven and adjust the temperature to 400 degrees F.
4. Set the timer for 15 minutes and press "Start/Stop" to begin preheating.
5. When the unit beeps to show that it is preheated, insert the air fry basket in the oven.
6. When the cooking time is complete, remove the air fry basket from the oven.
7. Serve warm.

Sweet & Spicy Parsnips

Servings: 5
Preparation Time: 15 minutes
Cooking Time: 44 minutes

Ingredients:

- 1½ pounds parsnip, peeled and cut into 1-inch chunks
- 1 tablespoon butter, melted
- 2 tablespoons honey
- 1 tablespoon dried parsley flakes, crushed
- ¼ teaspoon red pepper flakes, crushed
- Salt and ground black pepper, as required

Instructions:

1. In a large bowl, mix together the parsnips and butter.
2. Arrange the parsnip chunks into the greased air fry basket.
3. Select "Air Fry" of Breville Smart Air Fryer Oven and adjust the temperature to 355 degrees F.
4. Set the timer for 44 minutes and press "Start/Stop" to begin preheating.
5. When the unit beeps to show that it is preheated, insert the air fry basket in the oven.
6. Meanwhile, in a large bowl, mix together the remaining ingredients.
7. After 40 minutes of cooking, transfer the parsnips chunks into the bowl of honey mixture and toss to coat well.
8. Again, arrange the parsnip chunks in air fry basket and insert in the oven for about 4 minutes.
9. When the cooking time is complete, remove the air fry basket from the oven and transfer the chunks into a bowl.
10. Serve hot.

Tarragon Yellow Squash

Servings: 6
Preparation Time: 10 minutes
Cooking Time: 15 minutes

Ingredients:

- 4 teaspoons olive oil
- 2 pounds yellow squash, sliced
- 1 teaspoon kosher salt
- ½ teaspoon ground white pepper
- 1 tablespoon fresh tarragon leaves, chopped

Instructions:

1. In a large bowl, mix together the oil, yellow squash, salt and white pepper.
2. Arrange the yellow squash slices into the greased air fry basket.
3. Select "Air Fry" of Breville Smart Air Fryer Oven and adjust the temperature to 400 degrees F.
4. Set the timer for 15 minutes and press "Start/Stop" to begin preheating.
5. When the unit beeps to show that it is preheated, insert the air fry basket in the oven.
6. During cooking, toss the yellow squash 2-3 times.
7. When the cooking time is complete, remove the air fry basket from the oven and transfer the yellow squash into a bowl.
8. Add the tarragon leaves and mix till well.
9. Serve immediately.

Seasoned Zucchini

Servings: 6
Preparation Time: 10 minutes
Cooking Time: 10 minutes

Ingredients:

- 4 large zucchinis, cut into slices
- ¼ cup olive oil
- ½ of onion, sliced
- ¾ teaspoon Italian seasoning
- ½ teaspoon garlic salt
- ¼ teaspoon seasoned salt

Instructions:

1. In a large bowl, mix together all the ingredients.
2. Arrange the zucchini slices into the greased air fry basket.
3. Select "Air Fry" of Breville Smart Air Fryer Oven and adjust the temperature to 400 degrees F.
4. Set the timer for 10 minutes and press "Start/Stop" to begin preheating.
5. When the unit beeps to show that it is preheated, insert the air fry basket in the oven.
6. When the cooking time is complete, remove the air fry basket from the oven and transfer the zucchni into a bowl.
7. Serve immediately.

Glazed Mushrooms

Servings: 5
Preparation Time: 10 minutes
Cooking Time: 15 minutes

Ingredients:

- ½ cup low-sodium soy sauce
- 2 teaspoons honey
- 4 tablespoons balsamic vinegar
- 4 garlic cloves, finely chopped
- 2 teaspoons Chinese five-spice powder
- ½ teaspoon ground ginger
- 20 ounces fresh Cremini mushrooms, halved

Instructions:

1. In a bowl, add the soy sauce, honey, vinegar, garlic, five-spice powder and ground ginger and mix well. Set aside.
2. Place the mushroom into a greased baking dish in a single layer.
3. Select "Air Fry" of Breville Smart Air Fryer Oven and adjust the temperature to 350 degrees F.
4. Set the timer for 15 minutes and press "Start/Stop" to begin preheating.
5. When the unit beeps to show that it is preheated, arrange the baking dish over the wire rack.
6. After 10 minutes of cooking, in the baking dish, add the vinegar mixture and stir to combine.
7. When the cooking time is complete, remove the baking dish from oven.
8. Serve hot.

Wine Braised Mushrooms

Servings: 6
Preparation Time: 15 minutes
Cooking Time: 32 minutes

Ingredients:

- 1 tablespoon butter
- 2 teaspoons Herbs de Provence
- ½ teaspoon garlic powder
- 2 pounds fresh mushrooms, quartered
- 2 tablespoons white wine

Instructions:

1. In a frying pan, mix together the butter, herbs de Provence, and garlic powder over medium-low heat and stir fry for about 2 minutes.
2. Stir in the mushrooms and remove from the heat.
3. Transfer the mushroom mixture into a baking dish.
4. Select "Air Fry" of Breville Smart Air Fryer Oven and adjust the temperature to 320 degrees F.
5. Set the timer for 30 minutes and press "Start/Stop" to begin preheating.
6. When the unit beeps to show that it is preheated, arrange the baking dish over the wire rack.
7. After 25 minutes of cooking, stir the wine into mushroom mixture.
8. When the cooking time is complete, remove the baking dish from oven.
9. Serve hot.

Herbed Potatoes

Servings: 4
Preparation Time: 10 minutes
Cooking Time: 16 minutes

Ingredients:

*   6 small potatoes, chopped
*   3 tablespoons olive oil
*   2 teaspoons mixed dried herbs
*   Salt and ground black pepper, as required
*   2 tablespoons fresh parsley, chopped

Instructions:

1. In a large bowl, add the potatoes, oil, herbs, salt and black pepper and toss to coat well.
2. Arrange the potato pieces into the greased air fry basket.
3. Select "Air Fry" of Breville Smart Air Fryer Oven and adjust the temperature to 355 degrees F.
4. Set the timer for 16 minutes and press "Start/Stop" to begin preheating.
5. When the unit beeps to show that it is preheated, insert the air fry basket in the oven.
6. When the cooking time is complete, remove the air fry basket from the oven and transfer the potato into a bowl.
7. Garnish with parsley and serve.

Jacket Potatoes

Servings: 2
Preparation Time: 10 minutes
Cooking Time: 15 minutes

Ingredients:

*   2 potatoes
*   1 tablespoon mozzarella cheese, shredded
*   3 tablespoons sour cream
*   1 tablespoon butter, softened
*   1 teaspoon chives, minced
*   Salt and ground black pepper, as required

Instructions:

1. With a fork, prick the potatoes.
2. Arrange the potatoes into the greased air fry basket.
3. Select "Air Fry" of Breville Smart Air Fryer Oven and adjust the temperature to 355 degrees F.
4. Set the timer for 15 minutes and press "Start/Stop" to begin preheating.
5. When the unit beeps to show that it is preheated, insert the air fry basket in the oven.
6. Meanwhile, in a bowl, add the remaining ingredients and mix until well combined.
7. When the cooking time is complete, remove the air fry basket from the oven and transfer the potatoes onto a platter.
8. Open potatoes from the center and stuff them with cheese mixture.
9. Serve immediately

Feta Spinach

Servings: 6
Preparation Time: 10 minutes
Cooking Time: 15 minutes

Ingredients:

*   2 pounds fresh spinach, chopped
*   1 garlic clove, minced
*   1 jalapeño pepper, minced
*   4 tablespoons butter, melted
*   Salt and ground black pepper, as required
*   1 cup feta cheese, crumbled

- 1 teaspoon fresh lemon zest, grated

Instructions:

1. In a bowl, add the spinach, garlic, jalapeño, butter, salt and black pepper and mix well.
2. Arrange the spinach into the greased air fry basket.
3. Select "Air Fry" of Breville Smart Air Fryer Oven and adjust the temperature to 340 degrees F.
4. Set the timer for 15 minutes and press "Start/Stop" to begin preheating.
5. When the unit beeps to show that it is preheated, insert the air fry basket in the oven.
6. Meanwhile, in a bowl, add the remaining ingredients and mix until well combined.
7. When the cooking time is complete, remove the air fry basket from the oven and transfer the spinach into a bowl.
8. Immediately stir in the cheese and lemon zest.
9. Serve hot.

Cheesy Kale

Servings: 3
Preparation Time: 10 minutes
Cooking Time: 15 minutes

Ingredients:

- 1-pound fresh kale, tough ribs removed and chopped
- 3 tablespoons olive oil
- Salt and ground black pepper, as required
- 1 cup goat cheese, crumbled
- 1 teaspoon fresh lemon juice

Instructions:

1. In a bowl, add the kale, oil, salt and black pepper and mix well.
2. Arrange the kale into the greased air fry basket.
3. Select "Air Fry" of Breville Smart Air Fryer Oven and adjust the temperature to 340 degrees F.
4. Set the timer for 15 minutes and press "Start/Stop" to begin preheating.
5. When the unit beeps to show that it is preheated, insert the air fry basket in the oven.
6. Meanwhile, in a bowl, add the remaining ingredients and mix until well combined.

7. When the cooking time is complete, remove the air fry basket from the oven and immediately, transfer the kale mixture into a bowl.
8. Stir in the cheese and lemon juice and serve hot.

Beef, Pork & Lamb Recipes

Braised Beef Shanks

Servings: 4
Preparation Time: 15 minutes
Cooking Time: 6 hours

Ingredients:

- 2 pounds beef shanks
- 5 garlic cloves, minced
- 2 fresh rosemary sprigs
- 1 tablespoon fresh lime juice
- Salt and ground black pepper, as required
- 1 cup beef broth

Instructions:

1. Lightly grease a Dutch oven that will fit in the Breville Smart Air Fryer Oven.
2. In the pan, add all ingredients and mix well.
3. Arrange the Dutch oven over the wire rack.
4. Select "Slow Cooker" of Breville Smart Air Fryer Oven and set on "Low".
5. Set the timer for 6 hours and press "Start/Stop" to begin cooking.
6. When the cooking time is complete, remove the Dutch oven from the oven.
7. Open the lid and serve hot.

Spiced Beef Brisket

Servings: 12
Preparation Time: 15 minutes
Cooking Time: 6 hours

Ingredients:

- 1 tablespoon olive oil
- 1 large yellow onion, sliced
- 3 garlic cloves, minced
- 1 (4-pound) beef brisket
- ½ teaspoon red pepper flakes, crushed
- ½ teaspoon smoked paprika
- ½ teaspoon ground cumin
- Salt and ground black pepper, as required

- 2 cups beef broth

Instructions:

1. In an oven-safe pan that will fit in the Breville Smart Air Fryer Oven, place all ingredients and stir to combine.
2. Cover the pan with a lid.
3. Arrange the pan over the wire rack.
4. Select "Slow Cooker" of Breville Smart Air Fryer Oven and set on "Low".
5. Set the timer for 6 hours and press "Start/Stop" to begin cooking.
6. When the cooking time is complete, remove the pan from the oven and place the brisket onto a cutting board for about 10-15 minutes before slicing.
7. Cut into desired-sized slices and serve.

Balsamic Beef Top Roast

Servings: 10
Preparation Time: 10 minutes
Cooking Time: 45 minutes

Ingredients:

- 1 tablespoon butter, melted
- 1 tablespoon balsamic vinegar
- ½ teaspoon ground cumin
- ½ teaspoon smoked paprika
- ½ teaspoon red pepper flakes, crushed
- Salt and ground black pepper, as required
- 3 pounds beef top roast

Instructions:

1. In a bowl, add butter, vinegar, spices, salt and black pepper and mix well.
2. Coat the roast with spice mixture generously.
3. With kitchen twines, tie the roast to keep it compact.
4. Arrange the roast onto the enamel roasting pan.
5. Select "Air Fry" of Breville Smart Air Fryer Oven and adjust the temperature to 360 degrees F.
6. Set the timer for 45 minutes and press "Start/Stop" to begin preheating.
7. When the unit beeps to show that it is preheated, insert the roasting pan in the oven.

8. When the cooking time is complete, remove the roasting pan from the oven and place he roast onto a cutting board for about 10 minutes before slicing.
9. With a sharp knife, cut the roast into desired sized slices and serve.

Rosemary Beef Chuck Roast

Servings: 6
Preparation Time: 10 minutes
Cooking Time: 45 minutes

Ingredients:

- 1 (2-pound) beef chuck roast
- 1 tablespoon olive oil
- 2 teaspoons dried rosemary, crushed
- Salt, as required

Instructions:

1. In a bowl, add the oil, herbs and salt and mix well.
2. Coat the beef roast with herb mixture generously.
3. Arrange the beef roast onto the greased enamel roasting pan.
4. Select "Air Fry" of Breville Smart Air Fryer Oven and adjust the temperature to 360 degrees F.
5. Set the timer for 45 minutes and press "Start/Stop" to begin preheating.
6. When the unit beeps to show that it is preheated, insert the roasting pan in the oven.
7. When the cooking time is complete, remove the roasting pan from the oven and place the roast onto a cutting board.
8. With a piece of foil, cover the beef roast for about 20 minutes before slicing.
9. With a sharp knife, cut the beef roast into desired size slices and serve.

Beef Round Roast with Carrots

Servings: 6
Preparation Time: 15 minutes
Cooking Time: 8 hours

Ingredients:

- 1 (2-pound) beef round roast
- 3 large carrots, peeled and chopped

- 1 large yellow onion, sliced thinly
- 1 cup tomato sauce
- 1 teaspoon ground cumin
- ½ teaspoon ground cinnamon
- Salt and ground black pepper, as required

Instructions:

1. In an oven-safe pan that will fit in the Breville Smart Air Fryer Oven, place all ingredients and stir to combine.
2. Cover the pan with a lid.
3. Arrange the pan over the wire rack.
4. Select "Slow Cooker" of Breville Smart Air Fryer Oven and set on "Low".
5. Set the timer for 8 hours and press "Start/Stop" to begin cooking.
6. When the cooking time is complete, remove the pan from the oven and place the roast onto a cutting board for about 10-15 minutes before slicing.
7. Cut into desired-sized slices and serve.

Spiced Beef Sirloin Roast

Servings: 8
Preparation Time: 10 minutes
Cooking Time: 50 minutes

Ingredients:

- 1 tablespoon smoked paprika
- 1 teaspoon ground cumin
- 1 teaspoon garlic powder
- Salt and ground black pepper, as required
- 2½ pounds sirloin roast

Instructions:

1. In a bowl, mix together the spices, salt and black pepper.
2. Rub the roast with spice mixture generously.
3. Place the sirloin roast into the greased baking dish.
4. Select "Roast" of Breville Smart Air Fryer Oven and adjust the temperature to 350 degrees F.
5. Set the timer for 50 minutes and press "Start/Stop" to begin preheating.
6. When the unit beeps to show that it is preheated, arrange the baking dish over the wire rack.

7. When the cooking time is complete, remove the baking dish from oven and place the roast onto a platter for about 10 minutes before slicing.
8. With a sharp knife, cut the beef roast into desired sized slices and serve.

Simple Beef Tenderloin

Servings: 10
Preparation Time: 10 minutes
Cooking Time: 50 minutes

Ingredients:

- 1 (3½-pound) beef tenderloin, trimmed
- 2 tablespoons olive oil
- Salt and ground black pepper, as required

Instructions:

1. With kitchen twine, tie the tenderloin.
2. Rub the tenderloin with oil and season with salt and black pepper.
3. Place the tenderloin into the greased baking dish.
4. Select "Roast" of Breville Smart Air Fryer Oven and adjust the temperature to 400 degrees F.
5. Set the timer for 50 minutes and press "Start/Stop" to begin preheating.
6. When the unit beeps to show that it is preheated, arrange the baking dish over the wire rack.
7. When the cooking time is complete, remove the baking dish from oven and place the tenderloin onto a platter for about 10 minutes before slicing.
8. With a sharp knife, cut the tenderloin into desired sized slices and serve.

Bacon-Wrapped Filet Mignon

Servings: 2
Preparation Time: 10 minutes
Cooking Time: 15 minutes

Ingredients:

- 2 bacon slices
- 2 (4-ounce) filet mignon
- Salt and ground black pepper, as required
- Olive oil cooking spray

Instructions:

1. Wrap 1 bacon slice around each filet mignon and secure with toothpicks.
2. Season the filet mignon with the salt and black pepper lightly.
3. Arrange the filet mignon onto the wire rack and spray with cooking spray.
4. Select "Air Fry" of Breville Smart Air Fryer Oven and adjust the temperature to 375 degrees F.
5. Set the timer for 15 minutes and press "Start/Stop" to begin preheating.
6. When the unit beeps to show that it is preheated, insert the wire rack in the oven.
7. When the cooking time is complete, remove the rack from the oven.
8. Serve hot.

Seasoned Rib-Eye Steak

Servings: 3
Preparation Time: 10 minutes
Cooking Time: 14 minutes

Ingredients:

- 2 (8-ounce) rib-eye steaks
- 2 tablespoons olive oil
- 1 tablespoon simple steak seasoning
- Salt and ground black pepper, as required

Instructions:

1. Coat the steaks with oil and then sprinkle with seasoning, salt and black pepper evenly.
2. Arrange the steaks onto the enamel roasting pan.
3. Select "Bake" of Breville Smart Air Fryer Oven and adjust the temperature to 400 degrees F.
4. Set the timer for 14 minutes and press "Start/Stop" to begin preheating.
5. When the unit beeps to show that it is preheated, insert the roasting pan in the oven.
6. When the cooking time is complete, remove the roasting pan from the oven and place the steaks onto a cutting board for about 5 minutes.
7. Cut each steak into desired size slices and serve.

Spiced Flank Steak

Servings: 6
Preparation Time: 10 minutes
Cooking Time: 12 minutes

Ingredients:

- 2 tablespoons balsamic vinegar
- 2 tablespoons olive oil
- 3 garlic cloves, minced
- 1 teaspoon red chili powder
- 1 teaspoon ground cumin
- 1 teaspoon onion powder
- Salt and ground black pepper, as required
- 1 (2-pound) flank steak

Instructions:

1. In a large bowl, mix together the vinegar, spices, salt and black pepper.
2. Add the steak and coat with mixture generously.
3. Cover the bowl and place in the refrigerator for at least 1 hour.
4. Remove the steak from bowl and place onto the greased enamel roasting pan.
5. Select "Broil" of Breville Smart Air Fryer Oven and set the timer for 12 minutes.
6. Press "Start/Stop" to begin preheating.
7. When the unit beeps to show that it is preheated, insert the roasting pan in the oven.
8. When the cooking time is complete, remove the roasting pan from the oven and place the steak onto a cutting board.
9. With a sharp knife, cut the steak into desired sized slices and serve.

Buttered Striploin Steak

Servings: 2
Preparation Time: 10 minutes
Cooking Time: 12 minutes

Ingredients:

- 2 (7-ounces) striploin steaks
- 1½ tablespoons butter, softened
- Salt and ground black pepper, as required

Instructions:

1. Coat each steak evenly with butter and then, season with salt and black pepper.
2. Arrange the steaks into the greased air fry basket.
3. Select "Air Fry" of Breville Smart Air Fryer Oven and adjust the temperature to 392 degrees F.
4. Set the timer for 12 minutes and press "Start/Stop" to begin preheating.
5. When the unit beeps to show that it is preheated, insert the air fry basket in the oven.
6. When the cooking time is complete, remove the air fry basket from the oven and place the steaks onto serving plates.
7. Serve hot.

Simple Strip Steak

Servings: 2
Preparation Time: 10 minutes
Cooking Time: 8 minutes

Ingredients:

- 1 (9½-ounces) New York strip steak
- Salt and ground black pepper, as required
- 1 teaspoon olive oil

Instructions:

1. Coat the steak with oil and then, sprinkle with salt and black pepper evenly.
2. Arrange the steak onto the greased enamel roasting pan.
3. Select "Air Fry" of Breville Smart Air Fryer Oven and adjust the temperature to 400 degrees F.
4. Set the timer for 8 minutes and press "Start/Stop" to begin preheating.
5. When the unit beeps to show that it is preheated, insert the roasting pan in the oven.
6. When the cooking time is complete, remove the roasting pan from the oven and place the steak onto a platter for about 10 minutes.
7. Cut the steak into desired size slices and serve immediately.

Crispy Sirloin Steak

Servings: 2
Preparation Time: 15 minutes
Cooking Time: 10 minutes

Ingredients:

- 1 cup white flour
- 2 eggs
- 1 cup panko breadcrumbs
- 1 teaspoon garlic powder
- 1 teaspoon onion powder
- Salt and ground black pepper, as required
- 2 (6-ounces) sirloin steaks, pounded

Instructions:

1. In a shallow bowl, place the flour.
2. Crack the eggs in a second bowl and beat well.
3. In a third bowl, mix together the panko and spices.
4. Coat each steak with the white flour, then dip into beaten eggs and finally, coat with panko mixture.
5. Arrange the steak onto the greased enamel roasting pan.
6. Select "Air Fry" of Breville Smart Air Fryer Oven and adjust the temperature to 360 degrees F.
7. Set the timer for 10 minutes and press "Start/Stop" to begin preheating.
8. When the unit beeps to show that it is preheated, insert the roasting pan in the oven.
9. When the cooking time is complete, remove the roasting pan from the oven and transfer the steaks onto the serving plates.
10. Serve immediately.

Steak with Bell Peppers

Servings: 4
Preparation Time: 15 minutes
Cooking Time: 12 minutes

Ingredients:

- 1 teaspoon dried oregano, crushed
- 1 teaspoon onion powder
- 1 teaspoon garlic powder
- 1 teaspoon red chili powder
- 1 teaspoon paprika
- Salt, as required
- 1¼ pounds flank steak, cut into thin strips
- 3 green bell peppers, seeded and cubed
- 1 red onion, sliced
- 2 tablespoons olive oil
- 3-4 tablespoons feta cheese, crumbled

Instructions:

1. In a large bowl, mix together the oregano and spices.
2. Add the steak strips, bell peppers, onion, and oil and mix until well combined.
3. Arrange the steak mixture into the greased air fry basket.
4. Select "Air Fry" of Breville Smart Air Fryer Oven and adjust the temperature to 390 degrees F.
5. Set the timer for 12 minutes and press "Start/Stop" to begin preheating.
6. When the unit beeps to show that it is preheated, insert the air fry basket in the oven.
7. When the cooking time is complete, remove the air fry basket from the oven and place the steak mixture onto serving plates.
8. Serve immediately with the topping of feta.

Beef Jerky

Servings: 4
Preparation Time: 15 minutes
Cooking Time: 3 hours

Ingredients:

- 1½ pounds beef round, trimmed
- ½ cup Worcestershire sauce
- ½ cup low-sodium soy sauce
- 2 teaspoons honey
- 1 teaspoon liquid smoke
- 2 teaspoons onion powder
- ½ teaspoon red pepper flakes
- Ground black pepper, as required

Instructions:

1. In a zip-top bag, place the beef and freeze for 1-2 hours to firm up.

2. Place the meat onto a cutting board and cut against the grain into 1/8-¼-inch strips.
3. In a large bowl, add the remaining ingredients and mix until well combined.
4. Add the steak slices and coat with the mixture generously.
5. Refrigerate to marinate for about 4-6 hours.
6. Remove the beef slices from the bowl and with paper towels, pat dry them.
7. Divide the steak strips onto the enamel roasting pans and arrange in an even layer.
8. Select "Dehydrate" of Breville Smart Air Fryer Oven and adjust the temperature to 160 degrees F.
9. Set the timer for 3 hours and press "Start/Stop" to begin preheating.
10. When the unit beeps to show that it is preheated, insert 1 rack in the top position and another in the center position.
11. After 1½ hours, switch the position of roasting pans.
12. When the cooking time is complete, remove the trays from the oven.
13. Set the trays aside to cool completely before serving.

Beef & Tomato Curry

Servings: 8
Preparation Time: 15 minutes
Cooking Time: 5 hours

Ingredients:

- 2 pounds boneless beef, cubed
- 1½ cups fresh tomatoes, chopped finely
- 2 cups beef broth
- 1 cup unsweetened coconut milk
- Salt and ground black pepper, as required

Instructions:

1. In an oven-safe pan that will fit in the Breville Smart Air Fryer Oven, place all ingredients and stir to combine.
2. Cover the pan with a lid.
3. Arrange the pan over the wire rack.
4. Select "Slow Cooker" of Breville Smart Air Fryer Oven and set on "High".
5. Set the timer for 5 hours and press "Start/Stop" to begin cooking.

6. When the cooking time is complete, remove the pan from the oven.
7. Remove the lid and stir the mixture well.
8. Serve hot.

Cheesy Beef Soup

Servings: 8
Preparation Time: 15 minutes
Cooking Time: 5½ hours

Ingredients:

- 3 tablespoons butter
- 1 medium onion, chopped
- 2 celery stalks, chopped
- 2 large cloves garlic, minced
- 1-pound cooked beef, chopped
- 5 cups beef broth
- Salt and ground black pepper, as required
- 2 cups heavy cream
- 1½ cups Swiss cheese, shredded

Instructions:

1. In an oven-safe pan that will fit in the Breville Smart Air Fryer Oven, melt the butter over medium heat and sauté the onion, celery and garlic and cook for about 5 minutes.
2. Stir in the beef, broth, salt and black pepper and remove from the heat.
3. Cover the pan with a lid.
4. Arrange the pan over the wire rack.
5. Select "Slow Cooker" of Breville Smart Air Fryer Oven and set on "High".
6. Set the timer for 5½ hours and press "Start/Stop" to begin cooking.
7. After 4½ hours of cocking, stir in heavy cream and cheese.
8. When the cooking time is complete, remove the pan from the oven.
9. Open the lid and serve hot.

Meatballs in Sweet & Spicy Sauce

Servings: 8
Preparation Time: 20 minutes
Cooking Time: 30 minutes

Ingredients:

For Meatballs:

- 2 pounds lean ground beef
- 2/3 cup quick-cooking oats
- ½ cup Ritz crackers, crushed
- 1 (5-ounce) can evaporated milk
- 2 large eggs, beaten lightly
- 1 teaspoon honey
- 1 tablespoon dried onion, minced
- 1 teaspoon garlic powder
- 1 teaspoon ground cumin
- Salt and ground black pepper, as required

For Sauce:

- 1/3 cup orange marmalade
- 1/3 cup honey
- 1/3 cup brown sugar
- 2 tablespoons cornstarch
- 2 tablespoons soy sauce
- 1-2 tablespoons hot sauce
- 1 tablespoon Worcestershire sauce

Instructions:

1. For meatballs: in a large bowl, add all the ingredients and mix until well combined.
2. Make 1½-inch balls from the mixture.
3. Arrange the meatballs onto the enamel roasting pan in a single layer.
4. Select "Air Fry" of Breville Smart Air Fryer Oven and adjust the temperature to 380 degrees F.
5. Set the timer for 15 minutes and press "Start/Stop" to begin preheating.
6. When the unit beeps to show that it is preheated, insert the roasting pan in the oven.
7. Flip the meatballs once halfway through.
8. Meanwhile, for sauce: in a small pan, add all the ingredients over medium heat and cook until thickened, stirring continuously.
9. When the cooking time is complete, remove the roasting pan from the oven and transfer the meatballs onto a platter.
10. Serve the meatballs with the topping of sauce.

Beef Taco Casserole

Servings: 6
Preparation Time: 15 minutes
Cooking Time: 25 minutes

Ingredients:

- 2 pounds ground beef
- 2 tablespoons taco seasoning
- 1 cup cheddar cheese, shredded
- 1 cup cottage cheese
- 1 cup salsa

Instructions:

1. In a bowl, add the beef and taco seasoning and mix well.
2. Add the cheeses and salsa and stir to combine.
3. Place the beef mixture into a baking dish and slightly press to smooth the top surface.
4. Select "Bake" of Breville Smart Air Fryer Oven and adjust the temperature to 370 degrees F.
5. Set the timer for 25 minutes and press "Start/Stop" to begin preheating.
6. When the unit beeps to show that it is preheated, arrange the baking dish over the wire rack.
7. When the cooking time is complete, remove the baking dish from oven and set aside for about 5 minutes before serving.

Spiced Pork Shoulder

Servings: 6
Preparation Time: 15 minutes
Cooking Time: 55 minutes

Ingredients:

- 1 teaspoon ground cumin
- 1 teaspoon cayenne pepper
- ½ teaspoon garlic powder
- ½ teaspoon onion powder
- Salt and ground black pepper, as required
- 2 pounds skin-on pork shoulder

Instructions:

1. In a small bowl, place the spices, salt and black pepper and mix well.
2. Arrange the pork shoulder onto a cutting board, skin-side down.
3. Season the inner side of pork shoulder with salt and black pepper.
4. With kitchen twines, tie the pork shoulder into a long round cylinder shape.
5. Season the outer side of pork shoulder with spice mixture.
6. Arrange the pork shoulder into the greased enamel roasting pan.
7. Select "Roast" of Breville Smart Air Fryer Oven and adjust the temperature to 350 degrees F.
8. Set the timer for 55 minutes and press "Start/Stop" to begin preheating.
9. When the unit beeps to show that it is preheated, insert the roasting pan in the oven.
10. When the cooking time is complete, remove the roasting pan from the oven and place the pork shoulder onto a platter for about 10 minutes before slicing.
11. With a sharp knife, cut the pork shoulder into desired sized slices and serve.

Garlicky Pork Tenderloin

Servings: 5
Preparation Time: 15 minutes
Cooking Time: 20 minutes

Ingredients:

- 1½ pounds pork tenderloin
- Nonstick cooking spray
- 2 small heads roasted garlic
- Salt and ground black pepper, as required

Instructions:

1. Lightly spray all the sides of pork with cooking spray and then season with salt and black pepper.
2. Now, rub the pork with roasted garlic.
3. Arrange the roast onto the lightly greased enamel roasting pan.
4. Select "Air Fry" of Breville Smart Air Fryer Oven and adjust the temperature to 400 degrees F.

5. Set the timer for 20 minutes and press "Start/Stop" to begin preheating.
6. When the unit beeps to show that it is preheated, insert the roasting pan in the oven.
7. Flip the side of tenderloin once halfway through.
8. When the cooking time is complete, remove the roasting pan from the oven and place the tenderloin onto a platter for about 10 minutes before slicing.
9. With a sharp knife, cut the roast into desired sized slices and serve.

Maple Pork Tenderloin

Servings: 3
Preparation Time: 10 minutes
Cooking Time: 20 minutes

Ingredients:

- 2 tablespoons Sriracha
- 2 tablespoons maple syrup
- ¼ teaspoon red pepper flakes, crushed
- Salt, as required
- 1 pound pork tenderloin

Instructions:

1. In a small bowl, add the Sriracha, maple syrup, red pepper flakes and salt and mix well.
2. Arrange the pork tenderloin into the greased air fry basket.
3. Brush the pork tenderloin with mixture evenly.
4. Select "Air Fry" of Breville Smart Air Fryer Oven and adjust the temperature to 350 degrees F.
5. Set the timer for 20 minutes and press "Start/Stop" to begin preheating.
6. When the unit beeps to show that it is preheated, insert the air fry basket in the oven.
7. When the cooking time is complete, remove the air fry basket from the oven and place the pork tenderloin onto a platter for about 10 minutes before slicing.
8. With a sharp knife, cut the roast into desired sized slices and serve.

Honey Mustard Pork Tenderloin

Servings: 3
Preparation Time: 10 minutes
Cooking Time: 25 minutes

Ingredients:

- 1 pound pork tenderloin
- 1 tablespoon garlic, minced
- 2 tablespoons soy sauce
- 2 tablespoons honey
- 1 tablespoon Dijon mustard
- 1 tablespoon grain mustard
- 1 teaspoon Sriracha sauce

Instructions:

1. In a large bowl, add all the ingredients except pork and mix well.
2. Add the pork tenderloin and coat with the mixture generously.
3. Refrigerate to marinate for 2-3 hours.
4. Remove the pork tenderloin from bowl, reserving the marinade.
5. Place the pork tenderloin onto the lightly greased enamel roasting pan
6. Select "Air Fry" of Breville Smart Air Fryer Oven and adjust the temperature to 380 degrees F.
7. Set the timer for 25 minutes and press "Start/Stop" to begin preheating.
8. When the unit beeps to show that it is preheated, insert the roasting pan in the oven.
9. Flip the pork once halfway through and coat with the reserved marinade.
10. When the cooking time is complete, remove the roasting pan from the oven and place the pork tenderloin onto a platter for about 10 minutes before slicing.
11. With a sharp knife, cut the pork tenderloin into desired sized slices and serve.

Bacon-Wrapped Pork Tenderloin

Servings: 4
Preparation Time: 10 minutes
Cooking Time: 30 minutes

Ingredients:

- 1 (1½ pound) pork tenderloin
- 2 tablespoons Dijon mustard
- 1 tablespoon honey
- 4 bacon strips

Instructions:

1. Coat the tenderloin with mustard and honey.
2. Wrap the pork tenderloin with bacon strips.
3. Place the pork loin into a greased air fry basket.
4. Select "Air Fry" of Breville Smart Air Fryer Oven and adjust the temperature to 360 degrees F.
5. Set the timer for 30 minutes and press "Start/Stop" to begin preheating.
6. When the unit beeps to show that it is preheated, insert the air fry basket in the oven.
7. Flip the pork tenderloin once halfway through.
8. When the cooking time is complete, remove the air fry basket from the oven and place the pork loin onto a cutting board for about 10 minutes before slicing.
9. With a sharp knife, cut the tenderloin into desired sized slices and serve.

Seasoned Pork Loin

Servings: 6
Preparation Time: 10 minutes
Cooking Time: 30 minutes

Ingredients:

- 2 pounds pork loin
- 2 tablespoons olive oil, divided
- 2-3 tablespoons barbecue seasoning rub

Instructions:

1. Arrange a wire rack in a baking dish.
2. Coat the pork loin with oil and then rub with barbecue rub generously.
3. Arrange the pork loin into the prepared baking dish.
4. Select "Bake" of Breville Smart Air Fryer Oven and adjust the temperature to 350 degrees F.
5. Set the timer for 30 minutes and press "Start/Stop" to begin preheating.

6. When the unit beeps to show that it is preheated, arrange the baking dish over the wire rack.
7. When the cooking time is complete, remove the baking dish from oven and place the pork loin onto a cutting board.
8. With a piece of foil, cover the pork loin for about 10 minutes before slicing.
9. With a sharp knife, cut the pork loin into desired size slices and serve.

BBQ Pork Ribs

Servings: 4
Preparation Time: 15 minutes
Cooking Time: 26 minutes

Ingredients:

- ¼ cup honey, divided
- ¾ cup BBQ sauce
- 2 tablespoons tomato ketchup
- 1 tablespoon Worcestershire sauce
- 1 tablespoon soy sauce
- ½ teaspoon garlic powder
- Ground white pepper, as required
- 1¾ pounds pork ribs

Instructions:

1. In a bowl, mix together 3 tablespoons of honey and the remaining ingredients except pork ribs.
2. Add the pork ribs and coat with the mixture generously.
3. Refrigerate to marinate for about 20 minutes.
4. Arrange the ribs onto the greased enamel roasting pan.
5. Select "Air Fry" of Breville Smart Air Fryer Oven and adjust the temperature to 355 degrees F.
6. Set the timer for 26 minutes and press "Start/Stop" to begin preheating.
7. When the unit beeps to show that it is preheated, insert the roasting pan in the oven.
8. Flip the ribs once halfway through.
9. When the cooking time is complete, remove the roasting pan from the oven and transfer the ribs onto serving plates.
10. Drizzle with the remaining honey and serve immediately.

Simple Pork Chops

Servings: 4
Preparation Time: 10 minutes
Cooking Time: 12 minutes

Ingredients:

- 4 (6-ounce) boneless pork chops
- 1 tablespoon olive oil
- Salt and ground black pepper, as required

Instructions:

1. Coat both sides of the pork chops with the oil and then, rub with the salt and black pepper.
2. Place the pork chops onto the lightly greased enamel roasting pan.
3. Select "Air Fry" of Breville Smart Air Fryer Oven and adjust the temperature to 400 degrees F.
4. Set the timer for 12 minutes and press "Start/Stop" to begin preheating.
5. When the unit beeps to show that it is preheated, insert the roasting pan in the oven.
6. Flip the chops once halfway through.
7. When the cooking time is complete, remove the roasting pan from the oven.
8. Serve hot.

Seasoned Pork Chops

Servings: 4
Preparation Time: 10 minutes
Cooking Time: 12 minutes

Ingredients:

- 4 (6-ounce) boneless pork chops
- 2 tablespoons pork rub
- 1 tablespoon olive oil

Instructions:

1. Coat both sides of the pork chops with the oil and then, rub with the pork rub.
2. Place the pork chops onto the lightly greased enamel roasting pan.
3. Select "Air Fry" of Breville Smart Air Fryer Oven and adjust the temperature to 400 degrees F.

4. Set the timer for 12 minutes and press "Start/Stop" to begin preheating.
5. When the unit beeps to show that it is preheated, insert the roasting pan in the oven.
6. Flip the chops once halfway through.
7. When the cooking time is complete, remove the roasting pan from the oven.
8. Serve hot.

Spiced Pork Chops

Servings: 2
Preparation Time: 10 minutes
Cooking Time: 17 minutes

Ingredients:

- ½ cup panko breadcrumbs
- 1 teaspoon paprika
- ¼ teaspoon garlic powder
- ¼ teaspoon onion powder
- Salt and ground black pepper, as required
- 2 (5-ounce) boneless pork chops, trimmed
- Olive oil cooking spray

Instructions:

1. In a large shallow bowl, mix together the breadcrumbs and spices.
2. Coat the chops with breadcrumb mixture evenly.
3. Arrange the chops into the air fry basket and spray with cooking spray.
4. Select "Air Fry" of Breville Smart Air Fryer Oven and adjust the temperature to 360 degrees F.
5. Set the timer for 17 minutes and press "Start/Stop" to begin preheating.
6. When the unit beeps to show that it is preheated, insert the air fry basket in the oven.
7. Flip the chops once halfway through.
8. When the cooking time is complete, remove the air fry basket from the oven.
9. Serve hot.

Herbed Pork Chops

Servings: 4
Preparation Time: 15 minutes
Cooking Time: 12 minutes

Ingredients:

- 2 garlic cloves, minced
- ½ tablespoon fresh rosemary, chopped
- ½ tablespoon fresh parsley, chopped
- 2 tablespoons olive oil
- ¾ tablespoon Dijon mustard
- 1 tablespoon ground cumin
- 1 teaspoon sugar
- Salt and ground black pepper, as required
- 4 (6-ounces) (1-inch thick) pork chops

Instructions:

1. In a bowl, mix together the garlic, herbs, oil, mustard, cumin, sugar, and salt.
2. Add the pork chops and coat with marinade generously.
3. Cover the bowl and refrigerate for about 2-3 hours.
4. Remove the chops from the refrigerator and set aside at room temperature for about 30 minutes.
5. Arrange the chops onto the greased enamel roasting pan.
6. Select "Air Fry" of Breville Smart Air Fryer Oven and adjust the temperature to 390 degrees F.
7. Set the timer for 12 minutes and press "Start/Stop" to begin preheating.
8. When the unit beeps to show that it is preheated, insert the roasting pan in the oven.
9. Flip the chops once halfway through.
10. When the cooking time is complete, remove the roasting pan from the oven.
11. Serve hot.

Breaded Pork Chops

Servings: 2
Preparation Time: 15 minutes
Cooking Time: 28 minutes

Ingredients:

- 2 (5-ounce) boneless pork chops
- 1 cup buttermilk
- ½ cup flour
- 1 teaspoon garlic powder
- Salt and ground black pepper, as required
- Olive oil cooking spray

Instructions:

1. In a bowl, place the chops and buttermilk and refrigerate, covered for about 12 hours.
2. Remove the chops from the bowl of buttermilk, discarding the buttermilk.
3. In a shallow dish, mix together the flour, garlic powder, salt, and black pepper.
4. Coat the chops with flour mixture generously.
5. Place the pork chops onto the enamel roasting pan and spray with the cooking spray.
6. Select "Air Fry" of Breville Smart Air Fryer Oven and adjust the temperature to 380 degrees F.
7. Set the timer for 28 minutes and press "Start/Stop" to begin preheating.
8. When the unit beeps to show that it is preheated, insert the roasting pan in the oven.
9. Flip the chops once halfway through.
10. When the cooking time is complete, remove the roasting pan from the oven.
11. Serve hot.

Stuffed Pork Roll

Servings: 4
Preparation Time: 20 minutes
Cooking Time: 15 minutes

Ingredients:

- 1 scallion, chopped
- ¼ cup sun-dried tomatoes, chopped finely
- 2 tablespoons fresh parsley, chopped
- Salt and ground black pepper, as required
- 4 (6-ounce) pork cutlets, pounded slightly
- 2 teaspoons paprika
- ½ tablespoons olive oil

Instructions:

1. In a bowl, mix together the scallion, tomatoes, parsley, salt, and black pepper.
2. Spread the tomato mixture over each pork cutlet.
3. Roll each cutlet and secure with cocktail sticks.
4. Rub the outer part of rolls with paprika, salt and black pepper.
5. Coat the rolls with oil evenly.
6. Arrange pork rolls into the greased air fry basket in a single layer.
7. Select "Air Fry" of Breville Smart Air Fryer Oven and adjust the temperature to 390 degrees F.

8. Set the timer for 15 minutes and press "Start/Stop" to begin preheating.
9. When the unit beeps to show that it is preheated, insert the air fry basket in the oven.
10. When the cooking time is complete, remove the air fry basket from the oven and transfer the pork rolls onto serving plates.
11. Serve hot.

Pork with Mushrooms

Servings: 5
Preparation Time: 15 minutes
Cooking Time: 4 hours

Ingredients:

- 1 yellow onion, sliced
- 1½ pounds pork tenderloin, cut into slices
- ½ pound fresh button mushrooms, sliced
- 2 tablespoons olive oil
- Salt and ground black pepper, as required
- 2 cups chicken broth

Instructions:

1. Lightly grease a Dutch oven that will fit in the Breville Smart Air Fryer Oven.
2. In the bottom of pot, arrange the onion slices and top with the pork tenderloin, followed by the mushroom slices.
3. Sprinkle with salt and black pepper and pour the broth on top.
4. Arrange the Dutch oven over the wire rack.
5. Select "Slow Cooker" of Breville Smart Air Fryer Oven and set on "High".
6. Set the timer for 4 hours and press "Start/Stop" to begin cooking.
7. When the cooking time is complete, remove the Dutch oven from the oven.
8. Open the lid and stir the mixture.
9. Serve hot.

Pork Chili

Servings: 6
Preparation Time: 15 minutes
Cooking Time: 4 hours 10 minutes

Ingredients:

- ½ teaspoon olive oil
- 2 pounds lean ground pork
- 1 small onion, chopped
- 3 bell peppers, seeded and chopped
- 5 garlic cloves, minced
- 2 (14-ounce) cans diced tomatoes
- 1½ cups beef broth
- 2 tablespoons red chili powder
- ¼ teaspoon cayenne pepper
- ¼ teaspoon Italian seasoning
- Salt and ground black pepper, as required
- 1/3 cup cheddar cheese, shredded

Instructions:

1. In an oven-safe pan that will fit in the Breville Smart Air Fryer Oven, heat the oil over nedium heat and cook the pork for about 8-10 minutes.
2. Remove from the heat and stir in the remaining ingredients.
3. Cover the pan with a lid.
4. Arrange the pan over the wire rack.
5. Select "Slow Cooker" of Breville Smart Air Fryer Oven and set on "High".
6. Set the timer for 4 hours and press "Start/Stop" to begin cooking.
7. When the cooking time is complete, remove the pan from the oven.
8. Remove the lid and stir the mixture well.
9. Serve hot with the topping of cheddar cheese.

Pork Meatloaf

Servings: 8
Preparation Time: 15 minutes
Cooking Time: 1 hour 5 minutes

Ingredients:

For Meatloaf:

- 2 pounds lean ground turkey
- 1 cup quick-cooking oats
- ½ cup carrot, peeled and shredded
- 1 medium onion, chopped
- ½ cup fat-free milk
- ¼ of egg, beaten

- 2 tablespoons ketchup
- 1 teaspoon garlic powder
- ¼ teaspoon ground black pepper

For Topping:

- ¼ cup ketchup
- ¼ cup quick-cooking oats

Instructions:

1. For meatloaf: in a bowl, add all the ingredients and mix until well combined.
2. For topping: in another bowl, add all the ingredients and mix until well combined.
3. Transfer the mixture into a greased loaf pan and top with the topping mixture.
4. Select "Bake" of Breville Smart Air Fryer Oven and adjust the temperature to 350 degrees F.
5. Set the timer for 65 minutes and press "Start/Stop" to begin preheating.
6. When the unit beeps to show that it is preheated, arrange the loaf pan over the wire rack.
7. When the cooking time is complete, remove the loaf pan from oven and place the loaf pan onto a wire rack for about 10 minutes before slicing.
8. Carefully invert the loaf onto the wire rack.
9. Cut into desired sized slices and serve.

Feta Pork Meatballs

Servings: 8
Preparation Time: 20 minutes
Cooking Time: 24 minutes

Ingredients:

- 2 pounds ground pork
- 1 medium onion, chopped roughly
- ¼ cup fresh parsley, chopped roughly
- 4 garlic cloves, peeled
- ½ cup feta cheese, crumbled
- ½ cup Italian seasoned breadcrumbs
- 2 eggs, lightly beaten
- 1 tablespoon Worcestershire sauce
- Salt and ground black pepper, as required

Instructions:

1. In a mini food processor, add the onion, parsley and garlic and pulse until finely chopped.
2. Transfer the onion mixture into a large bowl.
3. Add the remaining ingredients and mix until well combined.
4. Make equal-sized balls from the mixture.
5. Arrange the meatballs into the greased air fry basket in a single layer.
6. Select "Air Fry" of Breville Smart Air Fryer Oven and adjust the temperature to 400 degrees F.
7. Set the timer for 12 minutes and press "Start/Stop" to begin preheating.
8. When the unit beeps to show that it is preheated, insert the air fry basket in the oven.
9. When the cooking time is complete, remove the air fry basket from the oven and transfer the meatballs onto a platter.
10. Serve hot.

Pork Stuffed Bell Peppers

Servings: 4
Preparation Time: 20 minutes
Cooking Time: 1 hour 10 minutes

Ingredients:

- 4 medium green bell peppers
- 2/3-pound ground pork
- 2 cups cooked white rice
- 1½ cups marinara sauce, divided
- 1 teaspoon Worcestershire sauce
- 1 teaspoon Italian seasoning
- Salt and ground black pepper, as required
- ½ cup mozzarella cheese, shredded

Instructions:

1. Cut the tops from bell peppers and then carefully remove the seeds.
2. Heat a large skillet over medium heat and cook the pork for bout 6-8 minutes, breaking into crumbles.
3. Add the rice, ¾ cup of marinara sauce, Worcestershire sauce, Italian seasoning, salt and black pepper and stir to combine.
4. Remove from the heat.
5. Arrange the bell peppers into the greased baking dish.

6. Carefully stuff each bell pepper with the pork mixture and top each with the remaining sauce.
7. Select "Bake" of Breville Smart Air Fryer Oven and adjust the temperature to 350 degrees F.
8. Set the timer for 60 minutes and press "Start/Stop" to begin preheating.
9. When the unit beeps to show that it is preheated, arrange the baking dish over the wire rack.
10. After 50 minutes of cooking, top each bell pepper with cheese.
11. When the cooking time is complete, remove the baking dish from oven.
12. Serve warm.

Glazed Ham

Servings: 6
Preparation Time: 10 minutes
Cooking Time: 40 minutes

Ingredients:

- 1½ pounds 2½ ounces ham
- 1 cup whiskey
- 2 tablespoons French mustard
- 2 tablespoons honey

Instructions:

1. Place the ham at room temperature for about 30 minutes before cooking.
2. In a bowl, mix together the whiskey, mustard, and honey.
3. Place the ham into the greased baking dish and coat with half of the honey mixture.
4. Select "Air Fry" of Breville Smart Air Fryer Oven and adjust the temperature to 320 degrees F.
5. Set the timer for 40 minutes and press "Start/Stop" to begin preheating.
6. When the unit beeps to show that it is preheated, arrange the baking dish over the wire rack.
7. After 25 minutes of cooking, turn the ham and top with the remaining honey mixture.
8. When the cooking time is complete, remove the baking dish from oven and place the ham onto a platter for about 10 minutes before slicing.
9. Cut the ham into desired size slices and serve.

Pork Sausage Casserole

Servings: 4
Preparation Time: 15 minutes
Cooking Time: 30 minutes

Ingredients:

- 6 ounces flour, sifted
- 2 eggs
- 1 red onion, thinly sliced
- 1 garlic clove, minced
- Salt and ground black pepper, as required
- ¾ cup milk
- 2/3 cup cold water
- 8 small sausages
- 8 fresh rosemary sprigs

Instructions:

1. In a bowl, mix together the flour, and eggs.
2. Add the onion, garlic, salt, and black pepper and mix them well.
3. Gently, add in the milk, and water and mix until well combined.
4. In each sausage, pierce 1 rosemary sprig.
5. Arrange sausages into the greased baking dish and top evenly with the flour mixture.
6. Select "Air Fry" of Breville Smart Air Fryer Oven and adjust the temperature to 320 degrees F.
7. Set the timer for 30 minutes and press "Start/Stop" to begin preheating.
8. When the unit beeps to show that it is preheated, arrange the baking dish over the wire rack.
9. When the cooking time is complete, remove the baking dish from oven.
10. Serve warm.

Garlicky Leg of Lamb

Servings: 10
Preparation Time: 15 minutes
Cooking Time: 8 hours

Ingredients:

- 3 pounds boneless leg of lamb, rolled
- 6 garlic cloves, minced
- Salt and ground black pepper, as required

- ½ cup chicken broth
- 2-3 tablespoon fresh lemon juice

Instructions:

1. In an oven-safe pan that will fit in the Breville Smart Air Fryer Oven, place all ingredients and stir to combine.
2. Cover the pan with a lid.
3. Arrange the pan over the wire rack.
4. Select "Slow Cooker" of Breville Smart Air Fryer Oven and set on "Low".
5. Set the timer for 8 hours and press "Start/Stop" to begin cooking.
6. When the cooking time is complete, remove the pan from the oven.
7. Remove the lid and place the leg of lamb onto a cutting board for about 10 minutes.
8. Cut the leg of lamb into desired-sized pieces and serve.

Herbed Leg of Lamb

Servings: 8
Preparation Time: 10 minutes
Cooking Time: 1¼ hours

Ingredients:

- 1 (2¼-pound) boneless leg of lamb
- 3 tablespoons olive oil
- Salt and ground black pepper, as required
- 2 fresh rosemary sprigs
- 2 fresh thyme sprigs

Instructions:

1. Rub the leg of lamb with oil and sprinkle with salt and black pepper.
2. Wrap the leg of lamb with herb sprigs.
3. Arrange the leg of lamb into the greased air fry basket.
4. Select "Air Fry" of Breville Smart Air Fryer Oven and adjust the temperature to 300 degrees F.
5. Set the timer for 75 minutes and press "Start/Stop" to begin preheating.
6. When the unit beeps to show that it is preheated, insert the air fry basket in the oven.
7. When the cooking time is complete, remove the air fry basket from the oven and place the leg of

lamb onto a cutting board for about 10 minutes before slicing.

8. Cut the leg of lamb into desired sized pieces and serve.

Leg of Lamb with Brussels Sprout

Servings: 6
Preparation Time: 15 minutes
Cooking Time: 1½ hours

Ingredients:

- 2¼ pounds leg of lamb
- 3 tablespoons olive oil, divided
- 1 tablespoon fresh rosemary, minced
- 1 tablespoon fresh lemon thyme
- 1 garlic clove, minced
- Salt and ground black pepper, as required
- 1½ pounds Brussels sprouts, trimmed
- 2 tablespoons honey

Instructions:

1. With a sharp knife, score the leg of lamb at several places.
2. In a bowl, mix together 2 tablespoons of oil, herbs, garlic, salt, and black pepper.
3. Generously coat the leg of lamb with oil mixture.
4. Place leg of lamb into the prepared air fry basket.
5. Select "Air Fry" of Breville Smart Air Fryer Oven and adjust the temperature to 300 degrees F.
6. Set the timer for 75 minutes and press "Start/Stop" to begin preheating.
7. When the unit beeps to show that it is preheated, insert the air fry basket in the oven.
8. Meanwhile, coat the Brussels sprout evenly with the remaining oil and honey.
9. When the cooking time is complete, remove the air fry basket from the oven.
10. Arrange the Brussels sprout into the air fry basket with leg of lamb.
11. Select "Air Fry" of Breville Smart Air Fryer Oven and adjust the temperature to 392 degrees F.
12. Set the timer for 15 minutes and press "Start/Stop" to begin cooking.
13. Insert the air fry basket in the oven.
14. When the cooking time is complete, remove the air fry basket from the oven and transfer the leg of lamb onto a platter.

15. With a piece of foil, cover the leg of lamb for about 10 minutes before slicing.
16. Cut the leg of lamb into desired size pieces and serve alongside the Brussels sprout.

Lamb Rump with Carrots

Servings: 4
Preparation Time: 15 minutes
Cooking Time: 35 minutes

Ingredients:

- 1 pounds 5-ounce lamb rump
- 2 garlic cloves, crushed
- 1 tablespoon dried rosemary, crushed
- 2 large carrots, peeled and cubed
- ½ of large yellow onion, peeled and halved
- 2 teaspoons olive oil

Instructions:

1. Rub the lamb with crushed garlic evenly and sprinkle with rosemary.
2. Place the the lamb rump into the greased air fry basket.
3. Select "Air Fry" of Breville Smart Air Fryer Oven and adjust the temperature to 355 degrees F.
4. Set the timer for 20 minutes and press "Start/Stop" to begin preheating.
5. When the unit beeps to show that it is preheated, insert the air fry basket in the oven.
6. Meanwhile, in a large bowl, add carrots, onions and oil and toss to coat well.
7. When the cooking time is complete, remove the air fry basket from the oven.
8. Place the carrot mixture on top of the lamb ramp.
9. Select "Air Fry" of Breville Smart Air Fryer Oven and adjust the temperature to 390 degrees F.
10. Set the timer for 15 minutes and press "Start/Stop" to begin cooking.
11. Insert the air fry basket in the oven.
12. When the cooking time is complete, remove the air fry basket from the oven and transfer the lamb rump onto a platter.
13. With a piece of foil, cover the leg of lamb for about 10 minutes before slicing.
14. Cut the lamb rumb into desired size pieces and serve alongside the carrot.

Herbed Rack of Lamb

Servings: 4
Preparation Time: 15 minutes
Cooking Time: 15 minutes

Ingredients:

- 4 tablespoons olive oil
- 2 teaspoons garlic, minced
- 2 tablespoons dried rosemary
- 1 tablespoon dried thyme
- Salt and ground black pepper, as required
- 1 rack of lamb

Instructions:

1. In a small bowl, add all the ingredients except for rackof lamb and mix well.
2. Rub the rack of lamb with herb muxure generously.
3. Arrange the rack of lamb into the greased air fry basket.
4. Select "Air Fry" of Breville Smart Air Fryer Oven and adjust the temperature to 360 degrees F.
5. Set the timer for 10 minutes and press "Start/Stop" to begin preheating.
6. When the unit beeps to show that it is preheated, insert the air fry basket in the oven.
7. When the cooking time is complete, remove the air fry basket from the oven and place the rack onto a cutting board for at least 10 minutes.
8. Cut the rack into individual chops and serve.

Crusted Rack of Lamb

Servings: 4
Preparation Time: 15 minutes
Cooking Time: 19 minutes

Ingredients:

- 1 rack of lamb, trimmed all fat and frenched
- Salt and ground black pepper, as required
- 1/3 cup pistachios, chopped finely
- 2 tablespoons panko breadcrumbs
- 2 teaspoons fresh thyme, chopped finely
- 1 teaspoon fresh rosemary, chopped finely
- 1 tablespoon butter, melted

- 1 tablespoon Dijon mustard

Instructions:

1. Season the rack with salt and black pepper evenly.
2. Arrange the rack into the greased enamel roasting pan.
3. Select "Air Fry" of Breville Smart Air Fryer Oven and adjust the temperature to 380 degrees F.
4. Set the timer for 12 minutes and press "Start/Stop" to begin preheating.
5. When the unit beeps to show that it is preheated, insert the roasting pan in the oven.
6. When the cooking time is complete, remove the roasting pan from the oven.
7. Meanwhile, in a small bowl, mix together the remaining ingredients except the mustard.
8. Brus the meaty side of the rack with the mustard.
9. Then, coat the pistachio mixture on all sides of the rack and press firmly.
10. Now, arrange the rack of lamb onto the roasting pan, meat side up.
11. Select "Air Fry" of Breville Smart Air Fryer Oven and adjust the temperature to 380 degrees F.
12. Set the timer for 7 minutes and press "Start/Stop" to begin preheating.
13. Insert the roasting pan in the oven.
14. When the cooking time is complete, remove the roasting pan from the oven and place the rack onto a cutting board for at least 10 minutes.
15. Cut the rack into individual chops and serve.

Crumbed Rack of Lamb

Servings: 5
Preparation Time: 15 minutes
Cooking Time: 30 minutes

Ingredients:

- 1 tablespoon butter, melted
- 1 garlic clove, finely chopped
- 1 (1¾-pound) rack of lamb
- Salt and ground black pepper, as required
- 1 egg
- ½ cup panko breadcrumbs
- 1 tablespoon fresh thyme, minced
- 1 tablespoon fresh rosemary, minced

Instructions:

1. In a bowl, mix together the butter, garlic, salt, and black pepper.
2. Coat the rack of lamb with garlic mixture evenly.
3. In a shallow dish, beat the egg.
4. In another dish, mix together the breadcrumbs and herbs.
5. Dip the rack of lamb in beaten egg and then, coat with breadcrumbs mixture.
6. Arrange the rack of lamb into the greased air fry basket.
7. Select "Air Fry" of Breville Smart Air Fryer Oven and adjust the temperature to 212 degrees F.
8. Set the timer for 25 minutes and press "Start/Stop" to begin preheating.
9. When the unit beeps to show that it is preheated, insert the air fry basket in the oven.
10. When the cooking time is complete, remove the air fry basket from the oven and place the rack onto a cutting board for at least 10 minutes.
11. Cut the rack into individual chops and serve.
12. After 25 minutes of cooking, set the temperatute of oven to 390 degrees F for 5 minutes.
13. When the cooking time is complete, remove the air fry basket from the oven and place the rack onto a cutting board for at least 10 minutes.
14. Cut the rack into individual chops and serve.

Herbed Lamb Loin Chops

Servings: 2
Preparation Time: 15 minutes
Cooking Time: 12 minutes

Ingredients:

* 4 (4-ounce) (½-inch thick) lamb loin chopped
* 1 teaspoon fresh thyme, minced
* 1 teaspoon fresh rosemary, minced
* 1 teaspoon fresh oregano, minced
* 2 garlic cloves, crushed
* Salt and ground black pepper, as required

Instructions:

1. In a large bowl, place all ingredients and mix well.
2. Refrigerate to marinate overnight.
3. Arrange the chops onto the greased enamel roasting pan.

4. Select "Bake" of Breville Smart Air Fryer Oven and adjust the temperature to 400 degrees F.
5. Set the timer for 12 minutes and press "Start/Stop" to begin preheating.
6. When the unit beeps to show that it is preheated, insert the roasting pan in the oven.
7. Flip the chops once halfway through.
8. When the cooking time is complete, remove the air fry basket from the oven and transfer the chops onto plates.
9. Serve hot.

Garlicky Lamb Loin Chops

Servings: 4
Preparation Time: 10 minutes
Cooking Time: 30 minutes

Ingredients:

* 3 garlic cloves, crushed
* 1 tablespoon fresh lemon juice
* 1 teaspoon olive oil
* 1 tablespoon Za'atar
* Salt and ground black pepper, as required
* 8 (3½-ounces) bone-in lamb loin chops, trimmed

Instructions:

1. In a large bowl, mix together the garlic, lemon juice, oil, Za'atar, salt, and black pepper.
2. Add the chops and generously coat with the mixture.
3. Arrange the lamb chops into the greased air fry basket.
4. Select "Air Fry" of Breville Smart Air Fryer Oven and adjust the temperature to 400 degrees F.
5. Set the timer for 15 minutes and press "Start/Stop" to begin preheating.
6. When the unit beeps to show that it is preheated, insert the air fry basket in the oven.
7. Flip the chops twice after every 5 minutes.
8. When the cooking time is complete, remove the air fry basket from the oven and transfer the chops onto plates.
9. Serve hot.

Maple Lamb Loin Chops

Servings: 2
Preparation Time: 10 minutes
Cooking Time: 15 minutes

Ingredients:

- 1 tablespoon Dijon mustard
- ½ tablespoon fresh lemon juice
- 1 teaspoon maple syrup
- 1 teaspoon canola oil
- ¼ teaspoon red pepper flakes, crushed
- Salt and ground black pepper, as required
- 4 (4-ounce) lamb loin chops

Instructions:

1. In a large bowl, mix together the mustard, lemon juice, oil, maple syrup, red pepper flakes, salt and black pepper.
2. Add the chops and coat with the mixture generously.
3. Place the chops onto the greased enamel roasting pan.
4. Select "Bake" of Breville Smart Air Fryer Oven and adjust the temperature to 390 degrees F.
5. Set the timer for 15 minutes and press "Start/Stop" to begin preheating.
6. When the unit beeps to show that it is preheated, insert the roasting pan in the oven.
7. Flip the chops once halfway through.
8. When the cooking time is complete, remove the air fry basket from the oven and transfer the chops onto plates.
9. Serve hot.

Mustard Lamb Loin Chops

Servings: 2
Preparation Time: 10 minutes
Cooking Time: 15 minutes

Ingredients:

- 1 tablespoon Dijon mustard
- ½ tablespoon white wine vinegar
- 1 teaspoon olive oil
- ½ teaspoon dried tarragon
- Salt and ground black pepper, as required
- 4 (4-ounce) lamb loin chops

Instructions:

1. In a large bowl, mix together the mustard, vinegar, oil, tarragon, salt, and black pepper.
2. Add the chops and coat with the mixture generously.
3. Arrange the chops onto the greased enamel roasting pan.
4. Select "Bake" of Breville Smart Air Fryer Oven and adjust the temperature to 390 degrees F.
5. Set the timer for 15 minutes and press "Start/Stop" to begin preheating.
6. When the unit beeps to show that it is preheated, arrange the roasting pan over the wire rack.
7. Flip the chops once halfway through.
8. When the cooking time is complete, remove the roasting pan from the oven and transfer the chops onto serving plates.
9. Serve hot.

Sweet & Sour Lamb Chops

Servings: 3
Preparation Time: 15 minutes
Cooking Time: 40 minutes

Ingredients:

- 3 (8-ounce) lamb shoulder chops
- Salt and ground black pepper, as required
- ¼ cup sugar
- 2 tablespoons fresh lime juice

Instructions:

1. Season the lamb chops with salt and black pepper generously.in a baking dish, place the chops and sprinkle with sugar, followed by the lime juice.
2. Arrange the chops onto the greased enemael roasting pan.
3. Select "Roast" of Breville Smart Air Fryer Oven and adjust the temperature to 376 degrees F.
4. Set the timer for 40 minutes and press "Start/Stop" to begin preheating.
5. When the unit beeps to show that it is preheated, insert the roasting pan in the oven.
6. After 20 minutes of cooking, flip the chops and coat with the pan juices.

7. When the cooking time is complete, remove the roasting pan from the oven and transfer the chops onto serving plates.
8. Serve hot.

Lamb Chops in Tomato Sauce

Servings: 4
Preparation Time: 15 minutes
Cooking Time: 8 hours

Ingredients:

- 1 pound lamb chops
- 1½ cups tomatoes, chopped finely
- 1 cup chicken broth
- Salt and ground black pepper, as required
- 3 tablespoon mixed fresh herbs (oregano, thyme, sage), chopped

Instructions:

1. In an oven-safe pan that will fit in the Breville Smart Air Fryer Oven, place all ingredients and stir to combine.
2. Cover the pan with a lid.
3. Arrange the pan over the wire rack.
4. Select "Slow Cooker" of Breville Smart Air Fryer Oven and set on "Low".
5. Set the timer for 8 hours and press "Start/Stop" to begin cooking.
6. When the cooking time is complete, remove the pan from the oven.
7. Remove the lid and stir the mixture well.
8. Serve hot.

Lamb Chops with Veggies

Servings: 4
Preparation Time: 15 minutes
Cooking Time: 8 minutes

Ingredients:

- 2 tablespoons fresh rosemary, minced
- 2 tablespoons fresh mint leaves, minced
- 1 garlic clove, minced
- 3 tablespoons olive oil
- Salt and ground black pepper, as required

- 4 (6-ounces) lamb chops
- 1 purple carrot, peeled and cubed
- 1 yellow carrot, peeled and cubed
- 1 parsnip, peeled and cubed
- 1 fennel bulb, cubed

Instructions:

1. In a large bowl, mix together the herbs, garlic, oil, salt, and black pepper.
2. Add the chops and generously coat with mixture.
3. Refrigerate to marinate for about 3 hours.
4. In a large pan of water, soak the vegetables for about 15 minutes.
5. Drain the vegetables completely.
6. Arrange chops into the greased air fry basket in a single layer.
7. Select "Air Fry" of Breville Smart Air Fryer Oven and adjust the temperature to 390 degrees F.
8. Set the timer for 10 minutes and press "Start/Stop" to begin preheating.
9. When the unit beeps to show that it is preheated, insert the air fry basket in the oven.
10. After 2 minutes of cooking, place the vegetables into the air fry basket and top with the chops in a single layer.
11. When the cooking time is complete, remove the air fry basket from the oven and transfer the chops and vegetables onto serving plates.
12. Serve hot.

Garlicky Lamb Steaks

Servings: 4
Preparation Time: 15 minutes
Cooking Time: 15 minutes

Ingredients:

- ½ onion, roughly chopped
- 5 garlic cloves, peeled
- 1 tablespoon fresh ginger, peeled
- 1 teaspoon ground fennel
- ½ teaspoon ground cumin
- ½ teaspoon ground cinnamon
- ½ teaspoon cayenne pepper
- Salt and ground black pepper, as required
- 1½ pounds boneless lamb sirloin steaks

Instructions:

1. In a blender, add the onion, garlic, ginger, and spices and pulse until smooth.
2. Transfer the mixture into a large bowl.
3. Add the lamb steaks and coat with the mixture generously.
4. Refrigerate to marinate for about 24 hours.
5. Arrange the lamb steaks into the greased air fry basket.
6. Select "Air Fry" of Breville Smart Air Fryer Oven and adjust the temperature to 330 degrees F.
7. Set the timer for 15 minutes and press "Start/Stop" to begin preheating.
8. When the unit beeps to show that it is preheated, insert the air fry basket in the oven.
9. Flip the steaks once halfway through.
10. When the cooking time is complete, remove the air fry basket from the oven and transfer the steaks onto plates.
11. Serve hot.

Lamb & Spinach Stew

Servings: 10
Preparation Time: 15 minutes
Cooking Time: 6 hours 10 minutes

Ingredients:

- ¼ cup olive oil, divided
- 2½ pounds lamb stew meat, cubed
- 1 teaspoon garlic powder
- Salt and ground black pepper, as required
- 2 small onions, chopped
- 1 teaspoon dried thyme, crushed
- 1 teaspoon dried oregano, crushed
- 1 teaspoon dried basil, crushed
- 1 cup carrot, peeled and chopped
- 1 celery stalk, chopped
- 10 cups fresh spinach, chopped
- 1 cup fresh tomatoes, chopped finely
- 2 cups chicken broth
- 3 tablespoons fresh lemon juice

Instructions:

1. In a Dutch oven that will fit in the Breville Smart Air Fryer Oven, heat 2 tablespoons of the oil over medium heat and cook the lamb cubes with garlic

powder, salt and black pepper for about 4-5 minutes.
2. With a slotted spoon, transfer the lamb into a bowl.
3. In the pot, add the remaining oil and onions and cook for about 4-5 minutes.
4. Remove from the heat and stir in the cooked lamb and remaining ingredients except for lemon juice.
5. Arrange the Dutch oven over the wire rack.
6. Select "Slow Cooker" of Breville Smart Air Fryer Oven and set on "Low".
7. Set the timer for 6 hours and press "Start/Stop" to begin cooking.
8. When the cooking time is complete, remove the Dutch oven from the oven.
9. Stir in the lemon juice and serve hot.

Lamb & Apricot Casserole

Servings: 4
Preparation Time: 15 minutes
Cooking Time: 8 hours 5 minutes

Ingredients:

- 1 teaspoon ground cumin
- 1 teaspoon ground coriander
- 1 teaspoon ground cinnamon
- 1 tablespoon olive oil
- 1-pound boneless lamb meat, trimmed and cubed
- 1½ cups tomato paste
- 1 medium onion, chopped finely
- 2 garlic cloves, minced
- 1 cup dried apricots

Instructions:

1. In a bowl, mix together the spices.
2. Add the lamb cubes and coat with the spice mixture evenly.
3. In a Dutch oven that will fit in the Breville Smart Air Fryer Oven, heat the oil over medium heat and cook the lamb cubes for about 4-5 minutes.
4. Remove from the heat and stir in the remaining ingredients.
5. Arrange the Dutch oven over the wire rack.
6. Select "Slow Cooker" of Breville Smart Air Fryer Oven and set on "Low".
7. Set the timer for 8 hours and press "Start/Stop" to begin cooking.

8. When the cooking time is complete, remove the Dutch oven from the oven and stir the mixture well.
9. Serve hot.

Lamb & Mushroom Chili

Servings: 6
Preparation Time: 15 minutes
Cooking Time: 8 hours 10 minutes

Ingredients:

- 1 pound ground lamb
- 1 tablespoon olive oil
- 1 medium onion, chopped finely
- 1 medium green bell pepper, seeded and chopped
- 8 ounces fresh mushrooms, sliced
- 3 small garlic cloves, minced
- 1 jalapeño pepper, seeded and chopped
- 1½ (14-ounces) cans diced tomatoes with juice
- 2 tablespoon red chili powder
- 1 teaspoon cayenne pepper
- Salt and ground black pepper, as required
- 1 cup beef broth
- ¼ cup fresh cilantro, chopped

Instructions:

1. In a Dutch oven that will fit in the Breville Smart Air Fryer Oven, heat the oil over medium heat and cook the ground lamb for about 4-5 minutes.
2. With a slotted spoon, transfer the lamb into a bowl.
3. In the pot, add the onion, bell pepper, mushrooms and garlic and sauté for about 5 minutes.
4. Remove from the heat and stir in the cooked lamb and remaining ingredients.
5. Arrange the Dutch oven over the wire rack.
6. Select "Slow Cooker" of Breville Smart Air Fryer Oven and set on "Low".
7. Set the timer for 8 hours and press "Start/Stop" to begin cooking.
8. When the cooking time is complete, remove the Dutch oven from the oven and stir the mixture well.
9. Serve hot.

Cheesy Lamb Burgers

Servings: 4
Preparation Time: 15 minutes
Cooking Time: 18 minutes

Ingredients:

For Burgers:

- 1 pound ground lamb
- ½ cup simple breadcrumbs
- ¼ cup red onion, chopped finely
- 3 tablespoons brown mustard
- 3 teaspoons low-sodium soy sauce
- 2 teaspoons fresh parsley, chopped finely
- Salt, to taste

For Topping:

- 2 tablespoons mustard
- 1 tablespoon brown sugar
- 1 teaspoon low-sodium soy sauce
- 4 Swiss cheese slices

Instructions:

1. For burgers: in a large bowl, add all the ingredients and mix until well combined.
2. Make 4 equal-sized patties from the mixture.
3. Arrange the patties onto the greased enamel roasting pan in a single layer.
4. Select "Air Fry" of Breville Smart Air Fryer Oven and adjust the temperature to 370 degrees F.
5. Set the timer for 15 minutes and press "Start/Stop" to begin preheating.
6. When the unit beeps to show that it is preheated, insert the roasting pan in the oven.
7. Flip the burgers once halfway through.
8. When the cooking time is complete, remove the roasting pan from the oven and coat the burgers with mustard mixture.
9. Arrange 1 cheese slice over each burger.
10. Again insert the roasting pan in the oven.
11. Select "Broil" and set the timer for 3 minutes.
12. Press "Start/Stop" to begin cooking.
13. When the cooking time is complete, remove the roasting pan from the oven and transfer the burgers onto serving plates.
14. Serve hot.

Herbed Lamb Meatballs

Servings: 8
Preparation Time: 15 minutes
Cooking Time: 7 hours 5 minutes

Ingredients:

- 2 pounds lean ground lamb
- 2 eggs, beaten
- 1 medium onion, chopped
- 2 tablespoons fresh cilantro, chopped
- 2 tablespoons fresh parsley leaves, chopped
- 1 tablespoon fresh mint leaves, chopped
- ½ teaspoon red pepper flakes, crushed
- ¼ teaspoon cayenne pepper
- ¼ teaspoon garlic powder
- Salt and ground black pepper, as required
- 3 tablespoons olive oil

Instructions:

1. In a large bowl, add all the ingredients except for oil and mix until well combined.
2. Make desired sized balls from mixture.
3. In an oven-safe pan that will fit in the Breville Smart Air Fryer Oven, heat the oil over medium heat and cook the meatballs for 4-5 minutes or until golden brown from all sides.
4. Remove from the heat and cover the pan with a lid.
5. Arrange the pan over the wire rack.
6. Select "Slow Cooker" of Breville Smart Air Fryer Oven and set on "Low".
7. Set the timer for 7 hours and press "Start/Stop" to begin cooking.
8. When the cooking time is complete, remove the pan from the oven.
9. Remove the lid and serve hot.

Poultry Recipes

Herbed Cornish Hen

Servings: 2
Preparation Time: 15 minutes
Cooking Time: 20 minutes

Ingredients:

- ¼ cup olive oil
- 1 teaspoon fresh rosemary, chopped
- 1 teaspoon fresh thyme, chopped
- 1 teaspoon fresh lemon zest, grated
- ¼ teaspoon red pepper flakes, crushed
- Salt and ground black pepper, as required
- 1 (1½-pound) Cornish game hen, backbone removed and halved

Instructions:

1. In a bowl, mix together the oil, herbs, lemon zest and spices.
2. Add the hen portions and coat with the marinade generously.
3. Cover the bowl and refrigerate for about 24 hours.
4. In a strainer, place the hen portions and set aside to drain any liquid.
5. Arrange the hen portions onto the greased wire rack.
6. Select "Air Fry" of Breville Smart Air Fryer Oven and adjust the temperature to 390 degrees F.
7. Set the timer for 20 minutes and press "Start/Stop" to begin preheating.
8. When the unit beeps to show that it is preheated, insert the wire rack in the oven.
9. When the cooking time is complete, remove the wire rack from the oven and place onto a platter for about 10 minutes before serving.

Herbed Whole Chicken

Servings: 6
Preparation Time: 15 minutes
Cooking Time: 1 hour 10 minutes

Ingredients:

- ¼ cup butter, softened

- 1 teaspoon dried rosemary, crushed
- 1 teaspoon dried basil, crushed
- 1 teaspoon dried oregano, crushed
- 1 teaspoon dried thyme, crushed
- 1 tablespoon garlic powder
- 1 tablespoon paprika
- 1 tablespoon ground cumin
- Salt and ground black pepper, as required
- 1 (3-pound) whole chicken, neck and giblets removed

Instructions:

1. In a bowl, add the butter, herbs, spices and salt and mix well.
2. Rub the chicken with spice mixture generously.
3. With kitchen twine, tie off wings and legs.
4. Arrange the chicken onto the greased enamel roasting pan.
5. Select "Bake" of Breville Smart Air Fryer Oven and adjust the temperature to 380 degrees F.
6. Set the timer for 70 minutes and press "Start/Stop" to begin preheating.
7. When the unit beeps to show that it is preheated, insert the roasting pan in the oven.
8. When the cooking time is complete, remove the roasting pan from the oven and place the chicken onto a platter for about 5-10 minutes before carving.
9. With a sharp knife, cut the chicken into desired sized pieces and serve.

Herbed Whole Chicken

Servings: 8
Preparation Time: 15 minutes
Cooking Time: 1 hour

Ingredients:

- 1 tablespoon fresh basil, chopped
- 1 tablespoon fresh oregano, chopped
- 1 tablespoon fresh thyme, chopped
- Salt and ground black pepper, as required
- 1 (4½-pound) whole chicken, necks and giblets removed
- 3 tablespoons olive oil, divided

Instructions:

1. In a bowl, mix together the herbs, salt and black pepper.
2. Coat the chicken with 2 tablespoons of oil and then, rub inside, outside and underneath the skin with half of the herb mixture generously.
3. Arrange the chicken into the greased air fry basket, breast-side down.
4. Select "Air Fry" of Breville Smart Air Fryer Oven and adjust the temperature to 360 degrees F.
5. Set the timer for 60 minutes and press "Start/Stop" to begin preheating.
6. When the unit beeps to show that it is preheated, insert the air fry basket in the oven.
7. After 30 minutes of cooking, arrange the chicken, breast-side up and oat with the remaining oil.
8. Then rub with the remaining herb mixture.
9. When the cooking time is complete, remove the air fry basket from the oven and place the chicken onto a cutting board for about 10 minutes before carving.
10. With a sharp knife, cut the chicken into desired sized pieces and serve.

Buttermilk Roasted Chicken

Servings: 5
Preparation Time: 15 minutes
Cooking Time: 20 minutes

Ingredients:

- 1 (3½ -pound) whole chicken, cut into 10 pieces
- Salt and ground black pepper, as required
- 2 cups buttermilk
- 2 cups all-purpose flour
- 1 tablespoon ground mustard
- 1 tablespoon garlic powder
- 1 tablespoon onion powder
- 1 tablespoon paprika
- 1 teaspoon cayenne pepper

Instructions:

1. Season the chicken pieces with salt and black pepper.
2. In a large bowl, add the chicken pieces and buttermilk and refrigerate to marinate for at least 1 hour.

3. Meanwhile, in a large bowl, add the flour, mustard, spices, salt and black pepper and mix well.
4. Arrange the chicken pieces into the greased air fry basket.
5. Select "Air Fry" of Breville Smart Air Fryer Oven and adjust the temperature to 390 degrees F.
6. Set the timer for 20 minutes and press "Start/Stop" to begin preheating.
7. When the unit beeps to show that it is preheated, insert the air fry basket in the oven and transfer the chicken pieces onto a platter.
8. Serve immediately.

Spicy Chicken Legs

Servings: 6
Preparation Time: 15 minutes
Cooking Time: 25 minutes

Ingredients:

- 2½ pounds chicken legs
- 2 tablespoons olive oil
- 1 teaspoon smoked paprika
- 1 teaspoon garlic powder
- ½ teaspoon ground cumin
- Salt and ground black pepper, as required

Instructions:

1. In a large bowl, add all the ingredients and mix well.
2. Arrange the chicken legs onto the greased enamel roasting pan.
3. Select "Air Fry" of Breville Smart Air Fryer Oven and adjust the temperature to 400 degrees F.
4. Set the timer for 25 minutes and press "Start/Stop" to begin preheating.
5. When the unit beeps to show that it is preheated, insert the roasting pan in the oven.
6. When the cooking time is complete, remove the roasting pan from the oven and transfer the chicken pieces onto a platter.
7. Serve hot.

Crispy Chicken Legs

Servings: 3
Preparation Time: 15 minutes
Cooking Time: 20 minutes

Ingredients:

- 3 (8-ounce) chicken legs
- 1 cup buttermilk
- 2 cups white flour
- 1 teaspoon garlic powder
- 1 teaspoon onion powder
- 1 teaspoon ground cumin
- 1 teaspoon paprika
- Salt and ground black pepper, as required
- 1 tablespoon olive oil

Instructions:

1. In a bowl, place the chicken legs and buttermilk and refrigerate for about 2 hours.
2. In a shallow dish, mix together the flour and spices.
3. Remove the chicken from buttermilk.
4. Coat the chicken legs with flour mixture, then dip into buttermilk and finally, coat with the flour mixture again.
5. Select "Air Fry" of Breville Smart Air Fryer Oven and adjust the temperature to 360 degrees F.
6. Set the timer for 20 minutes and press "Start/Stop" to begin preheating.
7. When the unit beeps to show that it is preheated, insert the air fry basket in the oven.
8. When the cooking time is complete, remove the air fry basket from the oven and transfer the chicken legs onto serving plates.
9. Serve hot.

Gingered Chicken Drumsticks

Servings: 3
Preparation Time: 10 minutes
Cooking Time: 25 minutes

Ingredients:

- ¼ cup full-fat coconut milk
- 2 teaspoons fresh ginger, minced

- 2 teaspoons galangal, minced
- 2 teaspoons ground turmeric
- Salt, as required
- 3 (6-ounce) chicken drumsticks

Instructions:

1. In a large bowl, add the coconut milk, galangal, ginger, and spices and mix well.
2. Add the chicken drumsticks and coat with the marinade generously.
3. Refrigerate to marinate for at least 6-8 hours.
4. Arrange the chicken drumsticks onto the greased enamel roasting pan.
5. Select "Air Fry" of Breville Smart Air Fryer Oven and adjust the temperature to 375 degrees F.
6. Set the timer for 25 minutes and press "Start/Stop" to begin preheating.
7. When the unit beeps to show that it is preheated, insert the roasting pan in the oven.
8. When the cooking time is complete, remove the roasting pan from the oven and transfer the chicken drumsticks onto plates.
9. Serve hot.

Herbed Chicken Drumsticks

Servings: 2
Preparation Time: 10 minutes
Cooking Time: 20 minutes

Ingredients:

- 1 tablespoon olive oil
- ½ teaspoon dried thyme, crushed
- ½ teaspoon dried rosemary, crushed
- ½ teaspoon oregano, crushed
- Salt and ground black pepper, as required
- 2 (6-ounce) chicken drumsticks

Instructions:

1. In a large bowl, place the oil, herbs, salt and black pepper and mix well.
2. Add the chicken drumsticks and coat with the mixture generously.
3. Place the chicken drumsticks into the greased baking dish.
4. Select "Air Fry" of Breville Smart Air Fryer Oven and adjust the temperature to 375 degrees F.

5. Set the timer for 20 minutes and press "Start/Stop" to begin preheating.
6. When the unit beeps to show that it is preheated, arrange the baking dish over the wire rack.
7. When the cooking time is complete, remove the baking dish from oven.
8. When the cooking time is complete, remove the roasting pan from the oven and transfer the chicken drumsticks onto plates.
9. Serve hot.

Glazed Chicken Drumsticks

Servings: 4
Preparation Time: 15 minutes
Cooking Time: 20 minutes

Ingredients:

- ¼ cup Dijon mustard
- 1 tablespoon maple syrup
- 2 tablespoons olive oil
- 1 tablespoon fresh rosemary, minced
- Salt and ground black pepper, as required
- 4 (6-ounce) chicken drumsticks

Instructions:

1. In bowl, add all ingredients except for drumsticks and mix until well combined.
2. Add the drumsticks and coat with the mixture generously.
3. Cover the bowl and refrigerate to marinate overnight.
4. Place the chicken drumsticks into the greased baking dish.
5. Select "Air Fry" of Breville Smart Air Fryer Oven and adjust the temperature to 320 degrees F.
6. Set the timer for 12 minutes and press "Start/Stop" to begin preheating.
7. When the unit beeps to show that it is preheated, arrange the baking dish over the wire rack.
8. After 12 minutes, flip the drumsticks and set the temperature to 390 degrees F for 8 minutes.
9. When the cooking time is complete, remove the roasting pan from the oven and transfer the chicken drumsticks onto plates.
10. Serve hot.

Simple Chicken Thighs

Servings: 4
Preparation Time: 10 minutes
Cooking Time: 20 minutes

Ingredients:

- 4 (4-ounces) skinless, boneless chicken thighs
- Salt and ground black pepper, as required
- 2 tablespoons butter, melted

Instructions:

1. Line a baking dish with a lightly greased piece of foil.
2. Rub the chicken thighs with salt and black pepper evenly and then, brush with melted butter.
3. Place the chicken thighs over the greased wire rack.
4. Select "Bake" of Breville Smart Air Fryer Oven and adjust the temperature to 450 degrees F.
5. Set the timer for 20 minutes and press "Start/Stop" to begin preheating.
6. When the unit beeps to show that it is preheated, place the chicken thighs over the greased wire rack.
7. When the cooking time is complete, remove the wire rack from oven and transfer the chicken thighs onto plates.
8. Serve hot.

Buttered Chicken Thighs

Servings: 2
Preparation Time: 10 minutes
Cooking Time: 20 minutes

Ingredients:

- 2 (4-ounces) skinless, boneless chicken thighs
- Salt and ground black pepper, as required
- 2 tablespoons butter, melted

Instructions:

1. Rub the chicken thighs with salt and black pepper evenly and then, brush with melted butter.

2. Place the chicken thighs into the greased baking dish.
3. Select "Bake" of Breville Smart Air Fryer Oven and adjust the temperature to 450 degrees F.
4. Set the timer for 20 minutes and press "Start/Stop" to begin preheating.
5. When the unit beeps to show that it is preheated, arrange the baking dish over the wire rack.
6. When the cooking time is complete, remove the wire rack from oven and transfer the chicken thighs onto plates.
7. Serve hot.

Lemony Chicken Thighs

Servings: 6
Preparation Time: 15 minutes
Cooking Time: 20 minutes

Ingredients:

- 6 (6-ounce) chicken thighs
- 2 tablespoons olive oil
- 2 tablespoons fresh lemon juice
- 1 tablespoon Italian seasoning
- Salt and ground black pepper, as required
- 1 lemon, sliced thinly

Instructions:

1. In a large bowl, add all the ingredients except for lemon slices and toss to coat well.
2. Refrigerate to marinate for 30 minutes to overnight.
3. Remove the chicken thighs from bowl and let any excess marinade drip off.
4. Arrange the chicken thighs onto the greased air fry basket.
5. Select "Air Fry" of Breville Smart Air Fryer Oven and adjust the temperature to 350 degrees F.
6. Set the timer for 20 minutes and press "Start/Stop" to begin preheating.
7. When the unit beeps to show that it is preheated, insert the air fry basket in the oven.
8. Flip the chicken thighs once halfway through.
9. When the cooking time is complete, remove the air fry basket from the oven and transfer the chicken thighs onto serving plates.
10. Serve hot alongside the lemon slices.

Herbed Chicken Thighs

Servings: 4
Preparation Time: 10 minutes
Cooking Time: 20 minutes

Ingredients:

- ½ tablespoon fresh rosemary, minced
- ½ tablespoon fresh thyme, minced
- Salt and ground black pepper, as required
- 4 (5-ounce) chicken thighs
- 2 tablespoons olive oil

Instructions:

1. In a large bowl, add the herbs, salt and black pepper and mix well.
2. Coat the chicken thighs with oil and then, rub with herb mixture.
3. Arrange the chicken thighs onto the greased enamel roasting pan.
4. Select "Air Fry" of Breville Smart Air Fryer Oven and adjust the temperature to 400 degrees F.
5. Set the timer for 20 minutes and press "Start/Stop" to begin preheating.
6. When the unit beeps to show that it is preheated, insert the roasting pan in the oven.
7. Flip the chicken thighs once halfway through.
8. When the cooking time is complete, remove the roasting pan from the oven and transfer the chicken thighs onto serving plates.
9. Serve hot.

Marinated Chicken Thighs

Servings: 4
Preparation Time: 10 minutes
Cooking Time: 30 minutes

Ingredients:

- 4 (6-ounce) bone-in, skin-on chicken thighs
- Salt and ground black pepper, as required
- ½ cup Italian salad dressing
- 1 teaspoon onion powder
- 1 teaspoon garlic powder

Instructions:

1. Season the chicken thighs with salt and black pepper evenly.
2. In a large bowl, add the chicken thighs and dressing and mix well.
3. Cover the bowl and refrigerate to marinate overnight.
4. Remove the chicken thighs from the bowl and place onto a plate.
5. Sprinkle the chicken thighs with onion powder and garlic powder.
6. Arrange the chicken thighs into the greased air fry basket.
7. Select "Air Fry" of Breville Smart Air Fryer Oven and adjust the temperature to 360 degrees F.
8. Set the timer for 30 minutes and press "Start/Stop" to begin preheating.
9. When the unit beeps to show that it is preheated, insert the air fry basket in the oven.
10. Flip the chicken thighs once halfway through.
11. When the cooking time is complete, remove the air fry basket from the oven and transfer the chicken thighs onto serving plates.
12. Serve hot.

Spiced Chicken Breasts

Servings: 4
Preparation Time: 10 minutes
Cooking Time: 35 minutes

Ingredients:

- 1½ tablespoons smoked paprika
- 1 teaspoon ground cumin
- Salt and ground black pepper, as required
- 2 (12-ounce) bone-in, skin-on chicken breasts
- 1 tablespoon olive oil

Instructions:

1. In a small bowl, mix together the paprika, cumin, salt and black pepper.
2. Coat the chicken breasts with oil evenly and then season with the spice mixture generously.
3. Arrange the chicken breasts into the greased air fry basket.
4. Select "Air Fry" of Breville Smart Air Fryer Oven and adjust the temperature to 375 degrees F.

5. Set the timer for 35 minutes and press "Start/Stop" to begin preheating.
6. When the unit beeps to show that it is preheated, insert the air fry basket in the oven.
7. Flip the chicken thighs once halfway through.
8. When the cooking time is complete, remove the air fry basket from the oven and transfer the chicken breasts onto a cutting board.
9. Cut each breast in 2 equal-sized pieces and serve.

Parmesan Chicken Breasts

Servings: 2
Preparation Time: 15 minutes
Cooking Time: 22 minutes

Ingredients:

* 2 (6-ounce) chicken breasts
* 1 egg, beaten
* 4 ounces breadcrumbs
* 1 tablespoon fresh basil
* 2 tablespoons olive oil
* ¼ cup pasta sauce
* ¼ cup Parmesan cheese, grated

Instructions:

1. In a shallow bowl, beat the egg.
2. In another bowl, add the oil, breadcrumbs, and basil and mix until a crumbly mixture forms.
3. Now, dip each chicken breast into the beaten egg and then, coat with the breadcrumb mixture.
4. Arrange the chicken breasts into the greased air fry basket.
5. Select "Air Fry" of Breville Smart Air Fryer Oven and adjust the temperature to 350 degrees F.
6. Set the timer for 22 minutes and press "Start/Stop" to begin preheating.
7. When the unit beeps to show that it is preheated, insert the air fry basket in the oven.
8. After 15 minutes of cooking, remove the basket from Air Fryer and spoon the pasta sauce over chicken breasts, followed by the cheese.
9. When the cooking time is complete, remove the air fry basket from the oven and transfer the chicken breasts onto serving plates.
10. Serve hot.

Crispy Chicken Breasts

Servings: 3
Preparation Time: 15 minutes
Cooking Time: 40 minutes

Ingredients:

* ¼ cup flour
* 1 large egg, beaten
* ¼ cup fresh cilantro, chopped
* 1 cup croutons, crushed
* 3 (5-ounce) boneless, skinless chicken breasts

Instructions:

1. In a shallow, dish place the flour.
2. In a second shallows dish, mix together the egg and cilantro.
3. In a third shallow dish, place croutons.
4. Coat the chicken breasts with flour, then dip into eggs and finally coat with croutons.
5. Arrange the chicken breasts onto the greased enamel roasting pan.
6. Select "Roast" of Breville Smart Air Fryer Oven and adjust the temperature to 375 degrees F.
7. Set the timer for 40 minutes and press "Start/Stop" to begin preheating.
8. When the unit beeps to show that it is preheated, insert the roasting pan in the oven.
9. When the cooking time is complete, remove the roasting pan from the oven and transfer the chicken breasts onto serving plates.
10. Serve hot.

Breaded Chicken Breasts

Servings: 6
Preparation Time: 15 minutes
Cooking Time: 12 minutes

Ingredients:

* 1 cup panko breadcrumbs
* ½ cup Parmesan cheese, grated
* ¼ cup fresh rosemary, minced
* ¼ teaspoon cayenne pepper
* Salt and ground black pepper, as required
* 6 (4-ounce) boneless, skinless chicken breasts

- 3 tablespoons olive oil
- Olive oil cooking spray

Instructions:

1. In a shallow dish, add the breadcrumbs, Parmesan cheese, rosemary, cayenne pepper, salt and black pepper and mix well.
2. Rub the chicken breasts with oil and then, coat with the breadcrumb's mixture evenly.
3. Arrange the chicken breasts onto the enamel roasting pan and spray with cooking spray.
4. Select "Air Fry" of Breville Smart Air Fryer Oven and adjust the temperature to 350 degrees F.
5. Set the timer for 12 minutes and press "Start/Stop" to begin preheating.
6. When the unit beeps to show that it is preheated, insert the roasting pan in the oven.
7. Flip the chicken breasts once halfway through.
8. When the cooking time is complete, remove the roasting pan from the oven and transfer the chicken breasts onto serving plates.
9. Serve hot.

Oat Crusted Chicken Breasts

Servings: 2
Preparation Time: 15 minutes
Cooking Time: 12 minutes

Ingredients:

- 2 (6-ounce) chicken breasts
- Salt and ground black pepper, as required
- ¾ cup oats
- 2 tablespoons mustard powder
- 1 tablespoon fresh parsley
- 2 medium eggs

Instructions:

1. Place the chicken breasts onto a cutting board and with a meat mallet, flatten each into even thickness.
2. Then, cut each breast in half.
3. Sprinkle the chicken pieces with salt and black pepper and set aside.
4. In a blender, add the oats, mustard powder, parsley, salt and black pepper and pulse until a coarse breadcrumb-like mixture is formed.

5. Transfer the oat mixture into a shallow bowl.
6. In another bowl, crack the eggs and beat well.
7. Coat the chicken with oats mixture and then, dip into beaten eggs and again, coat with the oats mixture.
8. Arrange chicken breasts into the greased baking dish in a single layer.
9. Select "Air Fry" of Breville Smart Air Fryer Oven and adjust the temperature to 350 degrees F.
10. Set the timer for 12 minutes and press "Start/Stop" to begin preheating.
11. When the unit beeps to show that it is preheated, arrange the baking dish over the wire rack.
12. Flip the chicken breasts once halfway through.
13. When the cooking time is complete, remove the baking dish from oven and transfer the chicken breasts onto a serving platter.
14. Serve hot.

Chicken Cordon Bleu

Servings: 2
Preparation Time: 15 minutes
Cooking Time: 30 minutes

Ingredients:

- 2 (6-ounce) boneless, skinless chicken breast halves, pounded into ¼-inch thickness
- 2 (¾-ounce) deli ham slices
- 2 Swiss cheese slices
- ½ cup all-purpose flour
- 1/8 teaspoon paprika
- Salt and ground black pepper, as required
- 1 large egg
- 2 tablespoons 2% milk
- ½ cup seasoned breadcrumbs
- 1 tablespoon olive oil
- 1 tablespoon butter, melted

Instructions:

1. Arrange the chicken breast halves onto a smooth surface.
2. Arrange 1 ham slice over each chicken breast half, followed by the cheese.
3. Roll up each chicken breast half and tuck in ends.
4. With toothpicks, secure the rolls.
5. In a shallow plate, mix together the flour, paprika, salt and black pepper.

6. In a shallow bowl, place the egg and milk and beat slightly.
7. In a third shallow plate, place the breadcrumbs.
8. Coat each chicken roll with flour mixture, then dip into egg mixture and finally coat with breadcrumbs.
9. In a small skillet, heat the oil over medium heat and cook the chicken rolls for about 3-5 minutes or until browned from all sides.
10. Transfer the chicken rolls into the greased baking dish.
11. Select "Bake" of Breville Smart Air Fryer Oven and adjust the temperature to 350 degrees F.
12. Set the timer for 25 minutes and press "Start/Stop" to begin preheating.
13. When the unit beeps to show that it is preheated, arrange the baking dish over the wire rack.
14. When the cooking time is complete, remove the baking dish from oven and transfer the chicken breasts onto a serving platter.
15. Discard the toothpicks and drizzle the chicken rolls with melted butter.
16. Serve immediately.

Stuffed Chicken Breasts

Servings: 2
Preparation Time: 15 minutes
Cooking Time: 30 minutes

Ingredients:

- 1 tablespoon olive oil
- 1¾ ounces fresh spinach
- ¼ cup ricotta cheese, shredded
- 2 (4-ounce) skinless, boneless chicken breasts
- Salt and ground black pepper, as required
- 2 tablespoons Parmesan cheese, grated
- ¼ teaspoon paprika

Instructions:

1. In a medium skillet, heat the oil over medium heat and cook the spinach for about 3-4 minutes.
2. Stir in the ricotta and cook for about 40-60 seconds.
3. Remove the skillet from heat and set aside to cool.
4. Cut slits into the chicken breasts about ¼-inch apart but not all the way through.
5. Stuff each chicken breast with the spinach mixture.

6. Season each chicken breast with salt and black pepper and then sprinkle the top with Parmesan cheese and paprika.
7. Arrange the chicken breasts into the greased air fry basket in a single layer.
8. Select "Air Fry" of Breville Smart Air Fryer Oven and adjust the temperature to 390 degrees F.
9. Set the timer for 25 minutes and press "Start/Stop" to begin preheating.
10. When the unit beeps to show that it is preheated, insert the air fry basket in the oven.
11. When the cooking time is complete, remove the air fry basket from the oven and transfer the chicken breasts onto a serving platter.
12. Serve hot.

Creamy Tomato Chicken

Servings: 4
Preparation Time: 15 minutes
Cooking Time: 6 hours

Ingredients:

- ¾ cup chicken broth
- 1 cup sour cream
- 1½ cups fresh tomatoes, chopped finely
- 1 jalapeño pepper, chopped finely
- 2 tablespoons fresh rosemary, chopped
- Salt and ground black pepper, as required
- 6 (4-ounce) boneless, skinless chicken breasts

Instructions:

1. Lightly grease a Dutch oven that will fit in the Breville Smart Air Fryer Oven.
2. In the Dutch oven, place all the ingredients and stir to combine.
3. Cover the Dutch oven with the lid.
4. Arrange the Dutch oven over the wire rack.
5. Select "Slow Cooker" of Breville Smart Air Fryer Oven and set on "Low".
6. Set the timer for 6 hours and press "Start/Stop" to begin cooking.
7. When the cooking time is complete, remove the Dutch oven from the oven.
8. Serve hot.

Chicken with Spinach & Mushrooms

Servings: 5
Preparation Time: 15 minutes
Cooking Time: 5 hours

Ingredients:

- 1½ pounds boneless chicken breasts, cut into thin strips
- 1½ cups fresh button mushrooms, sliced
- 2 cups fresh spinach, chopped
- 1 yellow onion, sliced thinly
- 1 cup chicken broth
- Pinch of cayenne pepper
- Salt and ground black pepper, as required

Instructions:

1. In an oven-safe pan that will fit in the Breville Smart Air Fryer Oven, place all ingredients and stir to combine.
2. Cover the pan with a lid.
3. Arrange the pan over the wire rack.
4. Select "Slow Cooker" of Breville Smart Air Fryer Oven and set on "Low".
5. Set the timer for 5 hours and press "Start/Stop" to begin cooking.
6. When the cooking time is complete, remove the pan from the oven.
7. Remove the lid and stir the mixture well.
8. Serve hot.

Chicken & Spinach Soup

Servings: 6
Preparation Time: 15 minutes
Cooking Time: 6 hours

Ingredients:

- 2 tablespoons unsalted butter, melted
- 4 cups cooked chicken, chopped
- 8 cups fresh spinach, chopped
- 1 large carrot, peeled and chopped
- 1 small onion, chopped finely
- ½ tablespoon garlic, minced
- Salt and ground black pepper, as required
- 6 cups chicken broth

Instructions:

1. In an oven-safe pan that will fit in the Breville Smart Air Fryer Oven, place all ingredients and stir to combine.
2. Cover the pan with a lid.
3. Arrange the pan over the wire rack.
4. Select "Slow Cooker" of Breville Smart Air Fryer Oven and set on "Low".
5. Set the timer for 6 hours and press "Start/Stop" to begin cooking.
6. When the cooking time is complete, remove the pan from the oven.
7. Remove the lid and serve hot.

Chicken Kabobs

Servings: 2
Preparation Time: 15 minutes
Cooking Time: 9 minutes

Ingredients:

- 1 (8-ounce) chicken breast, cut into medium-sized pieces
- 1 tablespoon fresh lemon juice
- 3 garlic cloves, grated
- 1 tablespoon fresh oregano, minced
- ½ teaspoon lemon zest, grated
- Salt and ground black pepper, as required
- 1 teaspoon plain Greek yogurt
- 1 teaspoon olive oil

Instructions:

1. In a large bowl, add the chicken, lemon juice, garlic, oregano, lemon zest, salt and black pepper and toss to coat well.
2. Cover the bowl and refrigerate overnight.
3. Remove the bowl from refrigerator and stir in the yogurt and oil.
4. Thread the chicken pieces onto the metal skewers.
5. Arrange the skewers into the greased air fry basket.
6. Select "Air Fry" of Breville Smart Air Fryer Oven and adjust the temperature to 350 degrees F.

7. Set the timer for 9 minutes and press "Start/Stop" to begin preheating.
8. When the unit beeps to show that it is preheated, insert the air fry basket in the oven.
9. Flip the skewers once halfway through.
10. When the cooking time is complete, remove the air fry basket from the oven and transfer the kabobs onto a serving platter.
11. Serve hot.

Rosemary Turkey Legs

Servings: 2
Preparation Time: 15 minutes
Cooking Time: 30 minutes

Ingredients:

- 2 garlic cloves, minced
- 1 tablespoon fresh rosemary, minced
- 1 teaspoon fresh lime zest, finely grated
- 2 tablespoons olive oil
- 1 tablespoon fresh lime juice
- Salt and ground black pepper, as required
- 2 turkey legs

Instructions:

1. in a large bowl, mix together the garlic, rosemary, lime zest, oil, lime juice, salt, and black pepper
2. Add the turkey legs and generously coat with marinade.
3. Refrigerate to marinate for about 6-8 hours.
4. Place turkey legs into the greased air fry basket.
5. Select "Air Fry" of Breville Smart Air Fryer Oven and adjust the temperature to 350 degrees F.
6. Set the timer for 30 minutes and press "Start/Stop" to begin preheating.
7. When the unit beeps to show that it is preheated, insert the air fry basket in the oven.
8. Flip the turkey legs once halfway through
9. When the cooking time is complete, remove the air fry basket from the oven and place the turkey legs onto the serving plates.
10. Serve hot.

BBQ Turkey Leg

Servings: 4
Preparation Time: 10 minutes
Cooking Time: 8 hours

Ingredients:

- 4 turkey legs
- Salt and ground black pepper, as required
- ¾ cup BBQ sauce
- 2 tablespoon prepared mustard
- 1/3 cup water

Instructions:

1. Season each turkey leg with salt and black pepper generously.
2. In a bowl, add remaining ingredients and mix until well combined.
3. Lightly grease an oven-safe pan that will fit in the Breville Smart Air Fryer Oven.
4. Cover the pan with a lid.
5. Arrange the pan over the wire rack.
6. Select "Slow Cooker" of Breville Smart Air Fryer Oven and set on "Low".
7. Set the timer for 8 hours and press "Start/Stop" to begin cooking.
8. When the cooking time is complete, remove the pan from the oven.
9. Remove the lid and serve hot.

Thyme Turkey Tenderloins

Servings: 4
Preparation Time: 6 minutes
Cooking Time: 23 minutes

Ingredients:

- 1 teaspoon dried thyme, crushed
- 1 teaspoon garlic powder
- Salt and ground black pepper, as required
- 1 (24-ounce) package boneless turkey breast tenderloins
- 2 tablespoon olive oil

Instructions:

1. In a small bowl, mix together the thyme, garlic powder, salt and black pepper.
2. Rub the turkey tenderloins with thyme mixture evenly.
3. In a large skillet, heat the oil over medium heat and cook the turkey tenderloins for about 10 minutes or until golden brown.
4. Remove from the heat and transfer the turkey tenderloins onto a baking dish.
5. Select "Bake" of Breville Smart Air Fryer Oven and adjust the temperature to 350 degrees F.
6. Set the timer for 10 minutes and press "Start/Stop" to begin preheating.
7. When the unit beeps to show that it is preheated, arrange the baking dish over the wire rack.
8. When the cooking time is complete, remove the baking dish from oven and transfer the turkey tenderloins onto serving plates.
9. Serve hot.

Simple Turkey Breast

Servings: 6
Preparation Time: 10 minutes
Cooking Time: 1 hour 20 minutes

Ingredients:

- 1 (2¾-pound) bone-in, skin-on turkey breast half
- Salt and ground black pepper, as required

Instructions:

1. Rub the turkey breast with the salt and black pepper evenly.
2. Arrange the turkey breast onto the greased enamel roasting pan.
3. Select "Bake" of Breville Smart Air Fryer Oven and adjust the temperature to 400 degrees F.
4. Set the timer for 80 minutes and press "Start/Stop" to begin preheating.
5. When the unit beeps to show that it is preheated, arrange the roasting pan over the wire rack.
6. When the cooking time is complete, remove the roasting pan from the oven and place the turkey breast onto a cutting board.
7. With a piece of foil, cover the turkey breast for about 20 minutes before slicing.

8. With a sharp knife, cut the turkey breast into desired size slices and serve.

Buttered Turkey Breast

Servings: 6
Preparation Time: 10 minutes
Cooking Time: 55 minutes

Ingredients:

- ¼ cup butter, softened
- 4 tablespoons fresh rosemary, chopped
- Salt and ground black pepper, as required
- 1 (4-pound) bone-in, skin-on turkey breast
- 2 tablespoons olive oil

Instructions:

1. In a bowl, add the butter, rosemary, salt and black pepper and mix well.
2. Rub the herb mixture under skin evenly.
3. Coat the outside of turkey breast with oil.
4. Place the turkey breast into the greased baking dish.
5. Select "Bake" of Breville Smart Air Fryer Oven and adjust the temperature to 350 degrees F.
6. Set the timer for 55 minutes and press "Start/Stop" to begin preheating.
7. When the unit beeps to show that it is preheated, arrange the baking dish over the wire rack.
8. When the cooking time is complete, remove the baking dish from oven and transfer the turkey breast onto a cutting board.
9. With a piece of foil, cover the turkey breast for about 20 minutes before slicing.
10. With a sharp knife, cut the turkey breast into desired-sized slices and serve.

Herbed & Spiced Turkey Breast

Servings: 6
Preparation Time: 15 minutes
Cooking Time: 40 minutes

Ingredients:

- ¼ cup butter, softened
- 2 tablespoons fresh rosemary, chopped

- 2 tablespoon fresh thyme, chopped
- 2 tablespoons fresh sage, chopped
- 2 tablespoons fresh parsley, chopped
- Salt and ground black pepper, as required
- 1 (4-pound) bone-in, skin-on turkey breast
- 2 tablespoons olive oil

Instructions:

1. In a bowl, add the butter, herbs, salt and black pepper and mix well.
2. Rub the herb mixture under skin evenly.
3. Coat the outside of turkey breast with oil.
4. Place the turkey breast into the greased baking dish.
5. Select "Bake" of Breville Smart Air Fryer Oven and adjust the temperature to 350 degrees F.
6. Set the timer for 40 minutes and press "Start/Stop" to begin preheating.
7. When the unit beeps to show that it is preheated, arrange the baking dish over the wire rack.
8. When the cooking time is complete, remove the baking dish from oven and transfer the turkey breast onto a cutting board.
9. With a piece of foil, cover the turkey breast for about 20 minutes before slicing.
10. With a sharp knife, cut the turkey breast into desired-sized slices and serve.

Glazed Turkey Breasts

Servings: 10
Preparation Time: 15 minutes
Cooking Time: 55 minutes

Ingredients:

- 1 (5-pound) boneless turkey breast
- Salt and ground black pepper, as required
- 3 tablespoons honey
- 2 tablespoon Dijon mustard
- 1 tablespoon butter, softened

Instructions:

1. Season the turkey breast with salt and black pepper generously and spray with cooking spray.
2. Arrange the turkey breast into the greased air fry basket.

3. Select "Air Fry" of Breville Smart Air Fryer Oven and adjust the temperature to 350 degrees F.
4. Set the timer for 55 minutes and press "Start/Stop" to begin preheating.
5. When the unit beeps to show that it is preheated, insert the air fry basket in the oven.
6. Meanwhile, for glaze: in a bowl, mix together the maple syrup, mustard and butter.
7. Flip the turkey breast twice, first after 25 minutes and then after 37 minutes.
8. After 50 minutes of cooking, coat the turkey breast with the glaze.
9. When the cooking time is complete, remove the air fry basket from oven and transfer the turkey breast onto a cutting board.
10. With a piece of foil, cover the turkey breast for about 10 minutes before slicing.
11. With a sharp knife, cut the turkey breast into desired-sized slices and serve.

Turkey Rolls

Servings: 3
Preparation Time: 20 minutes
Cooking Time: 40 minutes

Ingredients:

- 1 pound turkey breast fillet
- 1 garlic clove, crushed
- 1½ teaspoons ground cumin
- 1 teaspoon ground cinnamon
- ½ teaspoon red chili powder
- Salt, as required
- 2 tablespoons olive oil
- 3 tablespoons fresh parsley, chopped finely
- 1 small red onion, chopped finely

Instructions:

1. Place the turkey fillet on a cutting board.
2. Carefully cut horizontally along the length about 1/3 of way from the top, stopping about ¼-inch from the edge.
3. Open this part to have a long piece of fillet.
4. In a bowl, mix together the garlic, spices and oil.
5. In a small cup, reserve about 1 tablespoon of oil mixture.
6. In the remaining oil mixture, add the parsley and onion and mix well.
7. Coat the open side of fillet with onion mixture.

8. Roll the fillet tightly from the short side.
9. With a kitchen string, tie the roll at 1-1½-inch intervals.
10. Coat the outer side of roll with the reserved oil mixture.
11. Select "Air Fry" of Breville Smart Air Fryer Oven and adjust the temperature to 355 degrees F.
12. Set the timer for 40 minutes and press "Start/Stop" to begin preheating.
13. When the unit beeps to show that it is preheated, arrange the baking dish over the wire rack.
14. When the cooking time is complete, remove the baking dish from oven and place the turkey roll onto a cutting board for about 5-10 minutes before slicing.
15. With a sharp knife, cut the turkey roll into desired size slices and serve.

Turkey with Carrots

Servings: 10
Preparation Time: 15 minutes
Cooking Time: 1¼ hours

Ingredients:

- ¼ cup butter
- 5 carrots, peeled and cut into chunks
- 1 (6-pound) boneless turkey breast
- Salt and ground black pepper, as required
- 1 cup chicken broth

Instructions:

1. In a pan, heat the oil over medium heat and the carrots for about 4-5 minutes.
2. Add the turkey breast and cook for about 10 minutes or until golden brown from both sides.
3. Remove from the heat and stir in salt, black pepper and broth.
4. Transfer the mixture into a baking dish.
5. Select "Bake" of Breville Smart Air Fryer Oven and adjust the temperature to 375 degrees F.
6. Set the timer for 60 minutes and press "Start/Stop" to begin preheating.
7. When the unit beeps to show that it is preheated, arrange the baking dish over the wire rack.
8. When the cooking time is complete, remove the baking dish from oven.
9. With tongs, place the turkey onto a cutting board for about 5 minutes before slicing.

10. Cut into desired-sized slices and serve alongside carrots.

Turkey & Beans Chili

Servings: 6
Preparation Time: 15 minutes
Cooking Time: 5 hours 10 minutes

Ingredients:

- 1 tablespoon olive oil
- 1-pound lean ground turkey
- 1 red bell pepper, seeded and chopped
- 1 red onion, chopped finely
- 2 garlic cloves, minced
- 2 cups tomatoes, chopped finely
- 2 cups canned black beans, rinsed and drained
- 2 cups canned red kidney beans, rinsed and drained
- ½ cup tomato paste
- 1 teaspoon ground cumin
- 1 tablespoon chili powder
- ½ teaspoon garlic powder
- Salt and ground black pepper, as required
- 1 cup chicken broth
- ½ cup fresh cilantro, chopped

Instructions:

1. In a Dutch oven that will fit in the Breville Smart Air Fryer Oven, heat the oil over medium heat and cook the turkey for about 4-5 minutes.
2. Add the bell pepper, onion and garlic and cook for about 4-5 minutes.
3. Remove from the heat and stir in the remaining ingredients except for cilantro.
4. Arrange the Dutch oven over the wire rack.
5. Select "Slow Cooker" of Breville Smart Air Fryer Oven and set on "Low".
6. Set the timer for 5 hours and press "Start/Stop" to begin cooking.
7. When the cooking time is complete, remove the Dutch oven from the oven.
8. Remove the lid and serve hot with the topping of cilantro.

Turkey with Pumpkin

Servings: 2
Preparation Time: 15 minutes
Cooking Time: 3 hours

Ingredients:

- 8 ounces turkey breast, chopped
- 3½ ounce pumpkin, peeled and chopped
- ½ of small yellow onion, chopped
- ½ teaspoon ground cumin
- ½ teaspoon ground cinnamon
- ¼ teaspoon ground allspice
- Salt and ground black pepper, as required
- ½ cup chicken broth

Instructions:

1. Grease a Dutch oven that will fit in the Breville Smart Air Fryer Oven.
2. In the prepared pan, place all the ingredients and stir to combine.
3. Arrange the Dutch oven over the wire rack.
4. Select "Slow Cooker" of Breville Smart Air Fryer Oven and set on "High".
5. Set the timer for 3 hours and press "Start/Stop" to begin cooking.
6. When the cooking time is complete, remove the Dutch oven from the oven.
7. Remove the lid and serve hot.

Spiced Turkey Burgers

Servings: 6
Preparation Time: 15 minutes
Cooking Time: 8 minutes

Ingredients:

- 2 pounds ground turkey
- ½ tablespoon onion powder
- ½ tablespoon garlic powder
- ¼ teaspoon ground cumin
- Salt and ground black pepper, as required

Instructions:

1. In a bowl, add all the ingredients and mix well.
2. Make 6 equal-sized patties from the mixture.
3. Arrange the patties onto the greased enamel roasting pan in a single layer.
4. Select "Air Fry" of Breville Smart Air Fryer Oven and adjust the temperature to 360 degrees F.
5. Set the timer for 8 minutes and press "Start/Stop" to begin preheating.
6. When the unit beeps to show that it is preheated, insert the roasting pan in the oven.
7. Flip the burgers once halfway through.
8. When the cooking time is complete, remove the roasting pan from the oven and transfer the burgers onto serving plates.
9. Serve hot.

Ground Turkey with Olives

Servings: 8
Preparation Time: 15 minutes
Cooking Time: 4 hours 10 minutes

Ingredients:

- 1 teaspoon olive oil
- 2½ pounds ground turkey
- 1 cup red bell peppers, chopped
- 1 cup onion, minced
- 3 cloves garlic, minced
- ¼ cup fresh cilantro, minced
- 1 small tomato, chopped
- 8 ounces canned tomato sauce
- ¼ cup green olives, pitted
- 2 bay leaves
- 1½ teaspoons ground cumin
- ¼ teaspoon garlic powder
- Salt and ground black pepper, as required
- 1¼ cups water

Instructions:

1. In a Dutch oven that will fit in the Breville Smart Air Fryer Oven, heat the oil over medium heat and cook the turkey with salt and black pepper for about 5-6 minutes.
2. Add the bell pepper, onion and garlic and cook for about 3-4 minutes.

3. Remove from the heat and stir in the remaining ingredients.
4. Arrange the Dutch oven over the wire rack.
5. Select "Slow Cooker" of Breville Smart Air Fryer Oven and set on "High".
6. Set the timer for 4 hours and press "Start/Stop" to begin cooking.
7. When the cooking time is complete, remove the Dutch oven from the oven.
8. Remove the lid and discard the bay leaves.
9. Serve hot.

Thyme Duck Breast

Servings: 2
Preparation Time: 10 minutes
Cooking Time: 20 minutes

Ingredients:

- 1 cup beer
- 1 tablespoon olive oil
- 1 teaspoon mustard
- 1 tablespoon fresh thyme, chopped
- Salt and ground black pepper, as required
- 1 (10½-ounce) duck breast

Instructions:

1. In a bowl, place the beer, oil, mustard, thyme, salt, and black pepper and mix well
2. Add the duck breast and coat with marinade generously.
3. Cover the bowl and refrigerate for about 4 hours.
4. Remove from the refrigerator and with a piece of foil, cover the duck breast.
5. Arrange the foil cover duck breast into the air fry basket.
6. Select "Air Fry" of Breville Smart Air Fryer Oven and adjust the temperature to 390 degrees F.
7. Set the timer for 15 minutes and press "Start/Stop" to begin preheating.
8. When the unit beeps to show that it is preheated, insert the air fry basket in the oven.
9. When the cooking time is complete, remove the air fry basket from the oven.
10. Remove the foil from the duck breast and again arrange in the air fry basket.
11. Select "Air Fry" of Breville Smart Air Fryer Oven and adjust the temperature to 355 degrees F.
12. Set the timer for 5 minutes and press "Start/Stop" to begin cooking.
13. When the cooking time is complete, remove the air fry basket from the oven and place the duck breast onto a cutting board for about 5 minutes before slicing.
14. With a sharp knife, cut the duck breast into desired size slices and serve.

Garlicky Duck Legs

Servings: 2
Preparation Time: 10 minutes
Cooking Time: 30 minutes

Ingredients:

- 2 garlic cloves, minced
- 1 tablespoon fresh parsley, chopped
- 1 teaspoon five-spice powder
- Salt and ground black pepper, as required
- 2 duck legs

Instructions:

1. In a bowl, add the garlic, parsley, five-spice powder, salt and black pepper and mix until well combined.
2. Rub the duck legs with garlic mixture generously.
3. Arrange the duck legs onto the greased enamel roasting pan.
4. Select "Air Fry" of Breville Smart Air Fryer Oven and adjust the temperature to 340 degrees F.
5. Set the timer for 30 minutes and press "Start/Stop" to begin preheating.
6. When the unit beeps to show that it is preheated, insert the roasting pan in the oven.
7. When the cooking time is complete, remove the roasting pan from the oven and transfer the turkey legs onto serving plates.
8. Serve hot.

Fish & Seafood Recipes

Buttered Salmon

Servings: 2
Preparation Time: 10 minutes
Cooking Time: 10 minutes

Ingredients:

- 2 (6-ounce) salmon fillets
- Salt and ground black pepper, as required
- 1 tablespoon butter, melted

Instructions:

1. Season each salmon fillet with salt and black pepper and then, coat with the butter.
2. Arrange the salmon fillets into the greased air fry basket.
3. Select "Air Fry" of Breville Smart Air Fryer Oven and adjust the temperature to 360 degrees F.
4. Set the timer for 10 minutes and press "Start/Stop" to begin preheating.
5. When the unit beeps to show that it is preheated, insert the air fry basket in the oven.
6. When the cooking time is complete, remove the air fry basket from the oven and transfer the salmon fillets onto serving plates.
7. Serve hot.

Cajun Salmon

Servings: 2
Preparation Time: 10 minutes
Cooking Time: 7 minutes

Ingredients:

- 2 (7-ounce) (¾-inch thick) salmon fillets
- 1 tablespoon Cajun seasoning
- ½ teaspoon sugar
- 1 tablespoon fresh lemon juice

Instructions:

1. Sprinkle the salmon fillets with Cajun seasoning and sugar evenly.
2. Arrange the salmon fillets into the greased air fry basket, skin-side up.
3. Select "Air Fry" of Breville Smart Air Fryer Oven and adjust the temperature to 356 degrees F.
4. Set the timer for 7 minutes and press "Start/Stop" to begin preheating.
5. When the unit beeps to show that it is preheated, insert the air fry basket in the oven.
6. When the cooking time is complete, remove the air fry basket from the oven and transfer the salmon fillets onto serving plates.
7. Drizzle with the lemon juice and serve hot.

Spicy Salmon

Servings: 2
Preparation Time: 10 minutes
Cooking Time: 11 minutes

Ingredients:

- 1 teaspoon smoked paprika
- 1 teaspoon cayenne pepper
- 1 teaspoon onion powder
- 1 teaspoon garlic powder
- Salt and ground black pepper, as required
- 2 (6-ounce) (1½-inch thick) salmon fillets
- 2 teaspoons olive oil

Instructions:

1. In a bowl, add the spices and mix well.
2. Drizzle the salmon fillets with oil and then, rub with the spice mixture.
3. Arrange the salmon fillets into the greased air fry basket, skin-side up.
4. Select "Air Fry" of Breville Smart Air Fryer Oven and adjust the temperature to 390 degrees F.
5. Set the timer for 11 minutes and press "Start/Stop" to begin preheating.
6. When the unit beeps to show that it is preheated, insert the air fry basket in the oven.
7. When the cooking time is complete, remove the air fry basket from the oven and transfer the salmon fillets onto serving plates.
8. Serve hot.

Honey Glazed Salmon

Servings: 2
Preparation Time: 10 minutes
Cooking Time: 8 minutes

Ingredients:

- 2 (6-ounce) salmon fillets
- Salt, as required
- 2 tablespoons honey

Instructions:

1. Sprinkle the salmon fillets with salt and then, coat with honey.
2. Arrange the salmon fillets into the greased air fry basket, skin-side up.
3. Select "Air Fry" of Breville Smart Air Fryer Oven and adjust the temperature to 355 degrees F.
4. Set the timer for 8 minutes and press "Start/Stop" to begin preheating.
5. When the unit beeps to show that it is preheated, insert the air fry basket in the oven.
6. When the cooking time is complete, remove the air fry basket from the oven and transfer the salmon fillets onto serving plates.
7. Serve hot.

Crusted Salmon

Servings: 2
Preparation Time: 15 minutes
Cooking Time: 15 minutes

Ingredients:

- 2 (6-ounce) skinless salmon fillets
- Salt and ground black pepper, as required
- 3 tablespoons walnuts, chopped finely
- 3 tablespoons quick-cooking oats, crushed
- 2 tablespoons olive oil

Instructions:

1. Rub the salmon fillets with salt and black pepper evenly.
2. In a bowl, mix together the walnuts, oats and oil.
3. Arrange the salmon fillets onto the greased enamel roasting pan in a single layer.
4. Place the oat mixture over salmon fillets and gently, press down.
5. Select "Bake" of Breville Smart Air Fryer Oven and adjust the temperature to 400 degrees F.
6. Set the timer for 15 minutes and press "Start/Stop" to begin preheating.
7. When the unit beeps to show that it is preheated, insert the roasting pan in the oven.
8. When the cooking time is complete, remove the roasting pan from the oven and transfer the salmon fillets onto serving plates.
9. Serve hot.

Pesto Salmon

Servings: 4
Preparation Time: 15 minutes
Cooking Time: 15 minutes

Ingredients:

- 1¼ pounds salmon fillet, cut into 4 fillets
- 2 tablespoons white wine
- 1 tablespoon fresh lemon juice
- 2 tablespoons pesto, thawed
- 2 tablespoons pine nuts, toasted

Instructions:

1. Arrange the salmon fillets onto q foil-lined baking dish, skin-side down.
2. Drizzle the salmon fillets with wine and lemon juice.
3. Set aside for about 15 minutes.
4. Spread pesto over each salmon fillet evenly.
5. Arrange the salmon fillets into the greased baking dish.
6. Select "Broil" of Breville Smart Air Fryer Oven and then set the timer for 15 minutes.
7. Press "Start/Stop" to begin preheating.
8. When the unit beeps to show that it is preheated, arrange the baking dish over the wire rack.
9. When the cooking time is complete, remove the baking dish from oven and transfer the salmon fillets onto serving plates.
10. Garnish with toasted pine nuts and serve.

Lemony Salmon

Servings: 2
Preparation Time: 10 minutes
Cooking Time: 10 minutes

Ingredients:

- 1 tablespoon fresh lemon juice
- ½ tablespoons olive oil
- Salt and ground black pepper, as required
- 1 garlic clove, minced
- ½ teaspoon fresh thyme leaves, chopped
- 2 (7-ounce) salmon fillets

Instructions:

1. In a bowl, add all the ingredients except the salmon and mix well.
2. Add the salmon fillets and coat with the mixture generously.
3. Coat the fillets with flour mixture, then dip into egg mixture and finally coat with the cornflake mixture.
4. Arrange the salmon fillets onto a lightly greased wire rack, skin-side down.
5. Select "Air Fry" of Breville Smart Air Fryer Oven and adjust the temperature to 400 degrees F.
6. Set the timer for 10 minutes and press "Start/Stop" to begin preheating.
7. When the unit beeps to show that it is preheated, insert the wire rack in the oven.
8. Flip the salmon fillets once hallway through.
9. When the cooking time is complete, remove the salmon fillets from the oven and transfer onto serving plates.
10. Serve hot.

Salmon in Dill Sauce

Servings: 6
Preparation Time: 10 minutes
Cooking Time: 2 hours

Ingredients:

- 2 cups water
- 1 cup chicken broth
- 2 tablespoons fresh lemon juice

- ¼ cup fresh dill, chopped
- ½ teaspoon lemon zest, grated
- 6 (4-ounce) salmon fillets
- 1 teaspoon cayenne pepper
- Salt and ground black pepper, as required

Instructions:

1. In an oven-safe pan that will fit in the Breville Smart Air Fryer Oven, mix together the water, broth, lemon juice, lemon juice, dill and lemon zest.
2. Arrange the salmon fillets on top, skin side down and sprinkle with cayenne pepper, salt black pepper.
3. Cover the pan with a lid.
4. Arrange the pan over the wire rack.
5. Select "Slow Cooker" of Breville Smart Air Fryer Oven and set on "Low".
6. Set the timer for 2 hours and press "Start/Stop" to begin cooking.
7. When the cooking time is complete, remove the pan from the oven.
8. Remove the lid and serve hot.

Salmon with Broccoli

Servings: 2
Preparation Time: 15 minutes
Cooking Time: 12 minutes

Ingredients:

- 1½ cups small broccoli florets
- 2 tablespoons vegetable oil, divided
- Salt and ground black pepper, as required
- 1 (½-inch) piece fresh ginger, grated
- 1 tablespoon soy sauce
- 1 teaspoon rice vinegar
- 1 teaspoon light brown sugar
- ¼ teaspoon cornstarch
- 2 (6-ounce) skin-on salmon fillets
- 1 scallion, thinly sliced

Instructions:

1. In a bowl, mix together the broccoli, 1 tablespoon of oil, salt, and black pepper.

2. In another bowl, mix well the ginger, soy sauce, vinegar, sugar, and cornstarch.
3. Coat the salmon fillets with remaining oil and then with the ginger mixture.
4. Arrange the broccoli florets into the greased air fry basket and top with the salmon fillets.
5. Select "Air Fry" of Breville Smart Air Fryer Oven and adjust the temperature to 375 degrees F.
6. Set the timer for 12 minutes and press "Start/Stop" to begin preheating.
7. When the unit beeps to show that it is preheated, insert the air fry basket in the oven.
8. When the cooking time is complete, remove the air fry basket from the oven and transfer the salmon fillets and broccoli onto serving plates.
9. Serve hot.

Salmon Parcel

Servings: 2
Preparation Time: 15 minutes
Cooking Time: 23 minutes

Ingredients:

- 2 (4-ounce) salmon fillets
- 8 asparagus stalks
- ¼ cup white sauce
- 1 tablespoon oil
- ¼ cup champagne
- Salt and ground black pepper, as required

Instructions:

1. In a bowl, mix together all the ingredients.
2. Divide the salmon mixture over 2 pieces of foil evenly.
3. Seal the foil around the salmon mixture to form the packet.
4. Arrange the salmon parcels in air fry basket.
5. Select "Air Fry" of Breville Smart Air Fryer Oven and adjust the temperature to 355 degrees F.
6. Set the timer for 13 minutes and press "Start/Stop" to begin preheating.
7. When the unit beeps to show that it is preheated, insert the air fry basket in the oven.
8. When the cooking time is complete, remove the air fry basket from the oven and transfer the parcels onto serving plates.
9. Carefully open the parcels and serve hot.

Spiced Tilapia

Servings: 2
Preparation Time: 10 minutes
Cooking Time: 12 minutes

Ingredients:

- ½ teaspoon lemon pepper seasoning
- ½ teaspoon garlic powder
- 1/2 teaspoon onion powder
- Salt and ground black pepper, as required
- 2 (6-ounce) tilapia fillets
- 1 tablespoon olive oil

Instructions:

1. In a small bowl, mix together the spices, salt and black pepper.
2. Coat the tilapia fillets with oil and then rub with spice mixture.
3. Arrange the tilapia fillets onto a lightly greased wire rack, skin-side down.
4. Select "Air Fry" of Breville Smart Air Fryer Oven and adjust the temperature to 360 degrees F.
5. Set the timer for 12 minutes and press "Start/Stop" to begin preheating.
6. When the unit beeps to show that it is preheated, insert the wire rack in the oven.
7. Flip the tilapia fillets once hallway through.
8. When the cooking time is complete, remove the tilapia fillets from the oven and transfer onto serving plates.
9. Serve hot.

Ranch Tilapia

Servings: 4
Preparation Time: 10 minutes
Cooking Time: 13 minutes

Ingredients:

- ¾ cup cornflakes, crushed
- 1 (1-ounce) packet dry ranch-style dressing mix
- 2½ tablespoons vegetable oil
- 2 eggs
- 4 (6-ounce) tilapia fillets

Instructions:

1. In a shallow bowl, beat the eggs.
2. In another bowl, add the cornflakes, ranch dressing, and oil and mix until a crumbly mixture forms.
3. Dip the fish fillets into egg and then, coat with the breadcrumbs mixture.
4. Arrange the tilapia fillets into the greased air fry basket.
5. Select "Air Fry" of Breville Smart Air Fryer Oven and adjust the temperature to 356 degrees F.
6. Set the timer for 13 minutes and press "Start/Stop" to begin preheating.
7. When the unit beeps to show that it is preheated, insert the air fry basket in the oven.
8. When the cooking time is complete, remove the remove the tilapia fillets from the oven and transfer onto serving plates.
9. Serve hot.

Buttered Halibut

Servings: 4
Preparation Time: 15 minutes
Cooking Time: 30 minutes

Ingredients:

- 1 pound halibut fillets
- 1 tablespoon ginger paste
- 1 tablespoon garlic paste
- Salt and ground black pepper, as required
- 3 jalapeño peppers, chopped
- ¾ cup butter, chopped

Instructions:

1. Coat the halibut fillets with ginger-garlic paste and then season with salt and black pepper.
2. Arrange the halibut fillets into the greased air fry basket.
3. Select "Bake" of Breville Smart Air Fryer Oven and adjust the temperature to 380 degrees F.
4. Set the timer for 30 minutes and press "Start/Stop" to begin preheating.
5. When the unit beeps to show that it is preheated, insert the air fry basket in the oven.
6. When the cooking time is complete, remove the remove the halibut fillets from the oven and transfer onto serving plates.

7. Serve hot.

Glazed Halibut

Servings: 3
Preparation Time: 15 minutes
Cooking Time: 15 minutes

Ingredients:

- 1 garlic clove, minced
- ¼ teaspoon fresh ginger, finely grated
- ½ cup cooking wine
- ½ cup low-sodium soy sauce
- ¼ cup fresh orange juice
- 2 tablespoons fresh lime juice
- ¼ cup sugar
- ¼ teaspoon red pepper flakes, crushed
- 1 pound halibut steak

Instructions:

1. In a medium pan, add the garlic, ginger, wine, soy sauce, juices, sugar, and red pepper flakes and bring to a boil.
2. Cook for about 3-4 minutes, stirring continuously.
3. Remove the pan of marinade from heat and let it cool.
4. In a small bowl, add half of the marinade and reserve in a refrigerator.
5. In a resealable bag, add the remaining marinade and halibut steak.
6. Seal the bag and shake to coat well.
7. Refrigerate for about 30 minutes.
8. Place the halibut steak into the greased air fry basket.
9. Select "Air Fry" of Breville Smart Air Fryer Oven and adjust the temperature to 390 degrees F.
10. Set the timer for 11 minutes and press "Start/Stop" to begin preheating.
11. When the unit beeps to show that it is preheated, insert the air fry basket in the oven.
12. When the cooking time is complete, remove the remove the halibut steak from the oven and place onto a platter.
13. Cut the steak into 3 equal-sized pieces and coat with the remaining glaze.
14. Serve immediately.

Sweet & Sour Halibut

Servings: 4
Preparation Time: 10 minutes
Cooking Time: 12 minutes

Ingredients:

- 4 (5-ounce) halibut fillets
- 2 garlic cloves, minced
- 1 tablespoon fresh dill, minced
- 2 tablespoons butter, melted
- 2 tablespoons fresh lime juice
- ½ teaspoon honey
- ¼ teaspoon Sriracha

Instructions:

1. In a large resealable bag, place all the ingredients and seal the bag.
2. Shake the bag well to mix.
3. Place the bag in the refrigerator to marinate for at least 30 minutes.
4. Remove the fish fillets from the bag and shake off the excess marinade.
5. Arrange the halibut fillets onto the greased enamel roasting pan.
6. Select "Bake" of Breville Smart Air Fryer Oven and adjust the temperature to 400 degrees F.
7. Set the timer for 12 minutes and press "Start/Stop" to begin preheating.
8. When the unit beeps to show that it is preheated, arrange the roasting pan over the wire rack.
9. When the cooking time is complete, remove the roasting pan from the oven and transfer the fish fillets onto serving plates.
10. Serve hot.

Simple Haddock

Servings: 2
Preparation Time: 10 minutes
Cooking Time: 8 minutes

Ingredients:

- 2 (6-ounces) haddock fillets
- 1 tablespoon olive oil
- Salt and ground black pepper, as required

Instructions:

1. Coat the fish fillets with oil and then, sprinkle with salt and black pepper.
2. Arrange fish fillets into the greased air fry basket in a single layer.
3. Select "Air Fry" of Breville Smart Air Fryer Oven and adjust the temperature to 355 degrees F.
4. Set the timer for 8 minutes and press "Start/Stop" to begin preheating.
5. When the unit beeps to show that it is preheated, insert the air fry basket in the oven.
6. When the cooking time is complete, remove the remove the fish fillets from the oven and transfer onto serving plates.
7. Serve hot.

Haddock with Tomatoes & Bell Peppers

Servings: 4
Preparation Time: 15 minutes
Cooking Time: 4 hours

Ingredients:

- 1 (15-ounce) can diced tomatoes
- 1 green bell pepper, seeded and chopped
- 1 small onion, diced
- 1 garlic cloves, minced
- 1 pound haddock fillets
- 1 teaspoon dried herbs
- Salt and ground black pepper, as required
- 1/3 cup chicken broth

Instructions:

1. Lightly grease a Dutch oven that will fit in the Breville Smart Air Fryer Oven.
2. In the greased pot, place the tomatoes, bell pepper, onion and garlic and stir to combine.
3. Place the fish fillets on top of the tomato mixture and sprinkle with the herbs, salt and black pepper.
4. Place the broth on top evenly.
5. Arrange the Dutch oven over the wire rack.
6. Select "Slow Cooker" of Breville Smart Air Fryer Oven and set on "High".
7. Set the timer for 4 hours and press "Start/Stop" to begin cooking.

8. When the cooking time is complete, remove the Dutch oven from the oven.
9. Remove the lid and serve hot.

Glazed Hake

Servings: 2
Preparation Time: 10 minutes
Cooking Time: 12 minutes

Ingredients:

- ¼ cup soy sauce
- ¼ cup maple syrup
- 3 teaspoons rice wine vinegar
- 1 teaspoon water
- 4 (3½-ounce) hake fillets

Instructions:

1. In a small bowl, mix together the soy sauce, honey, vinegar, and water.
2. In another small bowl, reserve about half of the mixture.
3. Add the hake fillets in the remaining mixture and coat well.
4. Cover the bowl and refrigerate to marinate for about 2 hours.
5. Arrange the hake fillets into the greased air fry basket.
6. Select "Air Fry" of Breville Smart Air Fryer Oven and adjust the temperature to 355 degrees F.
7. Set the timer for 12 minutes and press "Start/Stop" to begin preheating.
8. When the unit beeps to show that it is preheated, insert the air fry basket in the oven.
9. Flip the hake fillets once halfway through and coat with the reserved marinade after every 3 minutes.
10. When the cooking time is complete, remove the remove the hake fillets from the oven and transfer onto serving plates.
11. Serve hot.

Tangy Sea Bass

Servings: 2
Preparation Time: 10 minutes
Cooking Time: 12 minutes

Ingredients:

- 2 (5-ounce) sea bass fillets
- 1 garlic clove, minced
- 1 teaspoon fresh dill, minced
- 1 tablespoon olive oil
- 1 tablespoon balsamic vinegar
- Salt and ground black pepper, as required

Instructions:

1. In a large resealable bag, add all the ingredients.
2. Seal the bag and shale well to mix.
3. Refrigerate to marinate for at least 30 minutes.
4. Remove the fish fillets from bag and shake off the excess marinade.
5. Arrange the fish fillets onto the greased enamel roasting pan in a single layer.
6. Select "Bake" of Breville Smart Air Fryer Oven and adjust the temperature to 450 degrees F.
7. Set the timer for 12 minutes and press "Start/Stop" to begin preheating.
8. When the unit beeps to show that it is preheated, insert the roasting pan in the oven.
9. Flip the fish fillets once halfway through.
10. When the cooking time is complete, remove the roasting pan from the oven and transfer the fish fillets onto serving plates.
11. Serve hot.

Simple Cod

Servings: 4
Preparation Time: 10 minutes
Cooking Time: 12 minutes

Ingredients:

- 4 (6-ounce) cod fillets
- Salt and ground black pepper, as required

Instructions:

1. Season the cod fillets with salt and black pepper evenly.
2. Arrange the cod fillets over the greased wire rack.
3. Select "Broil" of Breville Smart Air Fryer Oven and set the timer for 15 minutes.
4. Press "Start/Stop" to begin preheating.

5. When the unit beeps to show that it is preheated, insert the wire rack in the oven.
6. When the cooking time is complete, remove the wire rack from the oven and transfer the cod fillets onto serving plates.
7. Serve hot.

Crispy Cod

Servings: 4
Preparation Time: 15 minutes
Cooking Time: 15 minutes

Ingredients:

- 4 (4-ounce) (¾-inch thick) cod fillets
- Salt, as required
- 2 tablespoons all-purpose flour
- 2 eggs
- ½ cup panko breadcrumbs
- 1 teaspoon fresh dill, minced
- ½ teaspoon dry mustard
- ½ teaspoon lemon zest, grated
- ½ teaspoon onion powder
- ½ teaspoon paprika
- Olive oil cooking spray

Instructions:

1. Season the cod fillets with salt generously.
2. In a shallow bowl, place the flour.
3. Crack the eggs in a second bowl and beat well.
4. In a third bowl, mix together the panko, dill, lemon zest, mustard and spices.
5. Coat each cod fillet with the flour, then dip into beaten eggs and finally, coat with panko mixture.
6. Arrange the cod fillets into the air fry basket and spray the tops with cooking spray.
7. Select "Air Fry" of Breville Smart Air Fryer Oven and adjust the temperature to 400 degrees F.
8. Set the timer for 15 minutes and press "Start/Stop" to begin preheating.
9. When the unit beeps to show that it is preheated, insert the air fry basket in the oven.
10. Flip the cod fillets once hallway through.
11. When the cooking time is complete, remove the air fry basket from the oven and transfer the cod fillets onto serving plates.
12. Serve hot.

Cod with Asparagus

Servings: 1
Preparation Time: 10 minutes
Cooking Time: 15 minutes

Ingredients:

- 1 (6-ounce) cod fillet
- Salt and ground black pepper, as required
- 6 asparagus spears, trimmed
- 1 teaspoon olive oil
- 1 tablespoon fresh lemon juice

Instructions:

1. Season the cod fillet with salt and black pepper.
2. In a small bowl, add the asparagus, salt, black pepper and oil and toss to coat well.
3. Arrange the cod fillet into a greased baking dish on 1 side.
4. Arrange the asparagus spears alongside the cod fillet.
5. Select "Bake" of Breville Smart Air Fryer Oven and adjust the temperature to 450 degrees F.
6. Set the timer for 15 minutes and press "Start/Stop" to begin preheating.
7. When the unit beeps to show that it is preheated, arrange the baking dish over the wire rack.
8. When the cooking time is complete, remove the baking dish from oven and transfer the cod fillet and asparagus onto a serving plate.
9. Drizzle with lemon juice and serve immediately.

Cod Parcel

Servings: 2
Preparation Time: 15 minutes
Cooking Time: 20 minutes

Ingredients:

- 2 tablespoons butter, melted
- 1 tablespoon fresh lemon juice
- ½ teaspoon dried tarragon
- Salt and ground black pepper, as required
- ½ cup red bell peppers, seeded and thinly sliced
- ½ cup carrots, peeled and julienned
- ½ cup fennel bulbs, julienned

- 2 (5-ounce) frozen cod fillets, thawed
- 1 tablespoon olive oil

Instructions:

1. In a large bowl, mix together the butter, lemon juice, tarragon, salt, and black pepper.
2. Add the bell pepper, carrot, and fennel bulb and generously coat with the mixture.
3. Arrange 2 large parchment squares onto a smooth surface.
4. Coat the cod fillets with oil and then, sprinkle evenly with salt and black pepper.
5. Arrange 1 cod fillet onto each parchment square and top each evenly with the vegetables.
6. Top with any remaining sauce from the bowl.
7. Fold the parchment paper and crimp the sides to secure fish and vegetables.
8. Arrange the cod parcels into the air fry basket.
9. Select "Air Fry" of Breville Smart Air Fryer Oven and adjust the temperature to 350 degrees F.
10. Set the timer for 15 minutes and press "Start/Stop" to begin preheating.
11. When the unit beeps to show that it is preheated, insert the air fry basket in the oven.
12. When the cooking time is complete, remove the air fry basket from the oven and transfer the parcels onto serving plates.
13. Carefully open the parcels and serve hot.

Sardine in Tomato Gravy

Servings: 8
Preparation Time: 15 minutes
Cooking Time: 8 hours

Ingredients:

- 2 tablespoons olive oil
- 2 pounds fresh sardines, cubed
- 4 plum tomatoes, chopped finely
- 1 large onion, sliced
- 2 garlic cloves, minced
- 1 cup tomato puree
- Salt and ground black pepper, as required

Instructions:

1. In an oven-safe pan that will fit in the Breville Smart Air Fryer Oven, spread the oil evenly.

2. Place sardine over oil and top with the remaining all ingredients.
3. Cover the pan with a lid.
4. Arrange the pan over the wire rack.
5. Select "Slow Cooker" of Breville Smart Air Fryer Oven and set on "Low".
6. Set the timer for 8 hours and press "Start/Stop" to begin cooking.
7. When the cooking time is complete, remove the pan from the oven.
8. Remove the lid and serve hot.

Crusted Sole

Servings: 2
Preparation Time: 15 minutes
Cooking Time: 15 minutes

Ingredients:

- 2 teaspoons mayonnaise
- 1 teaspoon fresh chives, minced
- 3 tablespoons Parmesan cheese, shredded
- 2 tablespoons panko breadcrumbs
- Salt and ground black pepper, as required
- 2 (4-ounce) sole fillets

Instructions:

1. In a shallow plate, shallow plate, mix together the mayonnaise and chives.
2. In another shallow plate, mix together the cheese, breadcrumbs, salt and black pepper.
3. Coat the fish fillets with mayonnaise mixture and then roll in cheese mixture.
4. Arrange the sole fillets into the greased enamel roasting pan in a single layer.
5. Select "Bake" of Breville Smart Air Fryer Oven and adjust the temperature to 450 degrees F.
6. Set the timer for 15 minutes and press "Start/Stop" to begin preheating.
7. When the unit beeps to show that it is preheated, insert the roasting pan in the oven.
8. When the cooking time is complete, remove the roasting pan from the oven and transfer the sole fillets onto serving plates.
9. Serve hot.

Buttered Trout

Servings: 2
Preparation Time: 10 minutes
Cooking Time: 10 minutes

Ingredients:

- 2 (6-ounce) trout fillets
- Salt and ground black pepper, as required
- 1 tablespoon butter, melted

Instructions:

1. Season each trout fillet with salt and black pepper and then, coat with the butter.
2. Arrange the trout fillets onto the greased enamel roasting pan in a single layer.
3. Select "Air Fry" of Breville Smart Air Fryer Oven and adjust the temperature to 360 degrees F.
4. Set the timer for 10 minutes and press "Start/Stop" to begin preheating.
5. When the unit beeps to show that it is preheated, insert the roasting pan in the oven.
6. Flip the fillets once halfway through.
7. When the cooking time is complete, remove the roasting pan from the oven and transfer the trout fillets onto serving plates.
8. Serve hot.

Tuna Burgers

Servings: 4
Preparation Time: 15 minutes
Cooking Time: 6 minutes

Ingredients:

- 7 ounces canned tuna
- 1 large egg
- ¼ cup breadcrumbs
- 1 tablespoon mustard
- ¼ teaspoon garlic powder
- ¼ teaspoon onion powder
- ¼ teaspoon cayenne pepper
- Salt and ground black pepper, as required

Instructions:

1. In a bowl, add all the ingredients and mix until well combined.
2. Make 4 equal-sized patties from the mixture.
3. Arrange the patties onto the greased enamel roasting pan.
4. Select "Air Fry" of Breville Smart Air Fryer Oven and adjust the temperature to 400 degrees F.
5. Set the timer for 6 minutes and press "Start/Stop" to begin preheating.
6. When the unit beeps to show that it is preheated, insert the roasting pan in the oven.
7. Flip the burgers once halfway through.
8. When the cooking time is complete, remove the roasting pan from the oven and transfer the burgers onto serving plates.
9. Serve hot.

Prawn Burgers

Servings: 2
Preparation Time: 15 minutes
Cooking Time: 6 minutes

Ingredients:

- ½ cup prawns, peeled, deveined and chopped very finely
- ½ cup breadcrumbs
- 2-3 tablespoons onion, chopped finely
- ½ teaspoon ginger, minced
- ½ teaspoon garlic, minced
- ½ teaspoon red chili powder
- ½ teaspoon ground cumin
- ¼ teaspoon ground turmeric
- Salt and ground black pepper, as required

Instructions:

1. In a bowl, add all ingredients and mix until well combined.
2. Make small sized patties from mixture.
3. Arrange the patties into the greased air fry basket.
4. Select "Air Fry" of Breville Smart Air Fryer Oven and adjust the temperature to 355 degrees F.
5. Set the timer for 6 minutes and press "Start/Stop" to begin preheating.
6. When the unit beeps to show that it is preheated, insert the air fry basket in the oven.

7. When the cooking time is complete, remove the air fry basket from the oven and transfer the burgers onto serving plates.
8. Serve hot.

Prawns in Butter Sauce

Servings: 2
Preparation Time: 15 minutes
Cooking Time: 6 minutes

Ingredients:

- ½ pound large prawns, peeled and deveined
- 1 large garlic clove, minced
- 1 tablespoon butter, melted
- 1 teaspoon fresh lemon zest, grated

Instructions:

1. In a bowl, add all the ingredients and toss to coat well.
2. Set aside at room temperature for about 30 minutes.
3. Arrange the prawn mixture into a baking dish.
4. Select "Bake" of Breville Smart Air Fryer Oven and adjust the temperature to 450 degrees F.
5. Set the timer for 6 minutes and press "Start/Stop" to begin preheating.
6. When the unit beeps to show that it is preheated, arrange the baking dish over the wire rack.
7. When the cooking time is complete, remove the baking dish from the oven and transfer the shrimp onto serving plates.
8. Serve immediately.

Lemony Shrimp

Servings: 3
Preparation Time: 15 minutes
Cooking Time: 8 minutes

Ingredients:

- 2 tablespoons fresh lemon juice
- 1 tablespoon olive oil
- 1 teaspoon lemon pepper
- ¼ teaspoon paprika
- ¼ teaspoon garlic powder

- 12 ounces medium shrimp, peeled and deveined

Instructions:

1. In a large bowl, add all the ingredients except the shrimp and mix until well combined.
2. Add the shrimp and toss to coat well.
3. Arrange the shrimps onto the enamel roasting pan.
4. Select "Air Fry" of Breville Smart Air Fryer Oven and adjust the temperature to 400 degrees F.
5. Set the timer for 8 minutes and press "Start/Stop" to begin preheating.
6. When the unit beeps to show that it is preheated, insert the roasting pan in the oven.
7. When the cooking time is complete, remove the roasting pan from the oven and transfer the shrimp onto serving plates.
8. Serve hot.

Shrimp with Tomatoes

Servings: 4
Preparation Time: 15 minutes
Cooking Time: 7¼ hours

Ingredients:

- 1 (14–ounce) can peeled tomatoes, chopped finely
- 4 ounces canned tomato paste
- 2 garlic cloves, minced
- 2 tablespoons fresh parsley, chopped
- Salt and ground black pepper, as required
- 1 teaspoon lemon pepper
- 2 pounds cooked shrimp, peeled and deveined

Instructions:

1. In an oven-safe pan that will fit in the Breville Smart Air Fryer Oven, place all ingredients except for shrimp and stir to combine.
2. Cover the pan with a lid.
3. Arrange the pan over the wire rack.
4. Select "Slow Cooker" of Breville Smart Air Fryer Oven and set on "Low".
5. Set the timer for 7 hours and press "Start/Stop" to begin cooking.
6. When the cooking time is complete, remove the pan from the oven.
7. Remove the lid and stir in the shrimp.

8. Again arrange the pan over the wire rack.
9. Select "Slow Cooker" of Breville Smart Air Fryer Oven and set on "High".
10. Set the timer for 15 minutes and press "Start/Stop" to begin cooking.
11. When the cooking time is complete, remove the pan from the oven.
12. Remove the lid and stir and serve hot.

Shrimp Scampi

Servings: 3
Preparation Time: 20 minutes
Cooking Time: 7 minutes

Ingredients:

- 4 tablespoons salted butter
- 1 tablespoon fresh lemon juice
- 1 tablespoon garlic, minced
- 2 teaspoons red pepper flakes, crushed
- 1 pound shrimp, peeled and deveined
- 2 tablespoons fresh basil, chopped
- 1 tablespoon fresh chives, chopped
- 2 tablespoons dry white wine

Instructions:

1. Arrange a 7-inch round baking dish in the air fry basket.
2. Insert the basket in Breville Smart Air Fryer Oven.
3. Select "Air Fry" of Breville Smart Air Fryer Oven and adjust the temperature to 325 degrees F.
4. Set the timer for 7 minutes and press "Start/Stop" to begin preheating.
5. When the unit beeps to show that it is preheated, carefully remove the hot pan from Air fry basket.
6. In the heated pan, place butter, lemon juice, garlic, and red pepper flakes and stir to combine.
7. Return the pan into air fry basket and insert in the oven.
8. After 1 minute of cooking, stir the mixture once.
9. After 2 minutes of cooking, stir in the shrimp, basil, chives and wine.
10. While cooking, stir the mixture once after 5 minutes.
11. When the cooking time is complete, remove the air fry basket from the oven and place the pan onto a wire rack for about 1 minute.
12. Stir the mixture and transfer onto serving plates.

13. Serve hot.

Herbed Scallops

Servings: 2
Preparation Time: 15 minutes
Cooking Time: 4 minutes

Ingredients:

- ¾ pound sea scallops, cleaned and pat dry
- 1 tablespoon butter, melted
- ¼ tablespoon fresh thyme, minced
- ¼ tablespoon fresh rosemary, minced
- Salt and ground black pepper, as required

Instructions:

1. In a large bowl, place the scallops, butter, herbs, salt, and black pepper and toss to coat well.
2. Arrange the scallops into the greased air fry basket.
3. Select "Air Fry" of Breville Smart Air Fryer Oven and adjust the temperature to 390 degrees F.
4. Set the timer for 4 minutes and press "Start/Stop" to begin preheating.
5. When the unit beeps to show that it is preheated, insert the air fry basket in the oven.
6. When the cooking time is complete, remove the air fry basket from the oven.
7. Serve hot.

Scallops with Capers Sauce

Servings: 2
Preparation Time: 15 minutes
Cooking Time: 6 minutes

Ingredients:

- 10 (1-ounce) sea scallops, cleaned and patted very dry
- Salt and ground black pepper, as required
- ¼ cup extra-virgin olive oil
- 2 tablespoons fresh parsley, finely chopped
- 2 teaspoons capers, finely chopped
- 1 teaspoon fresh lemon zest, finely grated
- ½ teaspoon garlic, finely chopped

Instructions:

1. Season each scallop evenly with salt and black pepper.
2. Arrange scallops into the greased air fry basket in a single layer.
3. Select "Air Fry" of Breville Smart Air Fryer Oven and adjust the temperature to 400 degrees F.
4. Set the timer for 6 minutes and press "Start/Stop" to begin preheating.
5. When the unit beeps to show that it is preheated, insert the air fry basket in the oven.
6. Meanwhile, for the sauce: in a bowl, add the remaining ingredients and mix well.
7. When the cooking time is complete, remove the air fry basket from the oven and transfer the scallops onto serving plates.
8. Top with the sauce and serve immediately.

Creamy Mussels

Servings: 6
Preparation Time: 20 minutes
Cooking Time: 2 hours 20 minutes

Ingredients:

- 1 cup chicken broth
- 1 tablespoon red boat fish sauce
- 1 small yellow onion, chopped
- 2 garlic cloves, grated
- 1 lemongrass stalk, smashed
- 1 small Serrano pepper, chopped
- 2 pounds fresh mussels, scrubbed and debearded
- 1½ cups unsweetened coconut milk
- ¼ cup fresh cilantro leaves
- 1 teaspoon fresh lime zest, grated
- 1 tablespoon fresh lime juice

Instructions:

1. In an oven-safe pan that will fit in the Breville Smart Air Fryer Oven, add the broth, fish sauce, onion, garlic, lemongrass and serrano and stir to combine.
2. Cover the pan with a lid.
3. Arrange the pan over the wire rack.
4. Select "Slow Cooker" of Breville Smart Air Fryer Oven and set on "High".

5. Set the timer for 2 hours and 20 minutes and press "Start/Stop" to begin cooking.
6. When the cooking time is complete, remove the pan from the oven.
7. After 2 hours of cooking, stir in the mussels and coconut milk.
8. Remove the lid and stir in the cilantro, lime zest and juice.
9. Serve hot.

Buttered Crab Shells

Servings: 4
Preparation Time: 15 minutes
Cooking Time: 20 minutes

Ingredients:

- 4 soft crab shells, cleaned
- 1 cup buttermilk
- 3 eggs
- 2 cups panko breadcrumb
- 2 teaspoons seafood seasoning
- 1½ teaspoons lemon zest, grated
- 2 tablespoons butter, melted

Instructions:

1. In a shallow bowl, place the buttermilk.
2. In a second bowl, whisk the eggs.
3. In a third bowl, mix together the breadcrumbs, seafood seasoning, and lemon zest.
4. Soak the crab shells into the buttermilk for about 10 minutes.
5. Now, dip the crab shells into beaten eggs and then coat with the breadcrumb's mixture.
6. Arrange crab shells into the greased air fry basket in a single layer.
7. Select "Air Fry" of Breville Smart Air Fryer Oven and adjust the temperature to 375 degrees F.
8. Set the timer for 10 minutes and press "Start/Stop" to begin preheating.
9. When the unit beeps to show that it is preheated, insert the air fry basket in the oven.
10. When the cooking time is complete, remove the air fry basket from the oven and transfer the crab shells onto serving plates.
11. Drizzle the crab shells with the melted butter and serve immediately.

Crab Cakes

Servings: 4
Preparation Time: 15 minutes
Cooking Time: 10 minutes

Ingredients:

- ¼ cup red bell pepper, seeded and chopped finely
- 2 scallions, chopped finely
- 2 tablespoons mayonnaise
- 2 tablespoons breadcrumbs
- 1 tablespoon Dijon mustard
- 1 teaspoon old bay seasoning
- 8 ounces lump crabmeat, drained

Instructions:

1. In a large bowl, add all the ingredients except crabmeat and mix until well combined.
2. Gently fold in the crabmeat.
3. Make 4 equal-sized patties from the mixture.
4. Arrange the patties onto a lightly greased enamel roasting pan.
5. Select "Air Fry" of Breville Smart Air Fryer Oven and adjust the temperature to 370 degrees F.
6. Set the timer for 10 minutes and press "Start/Stop" to begin preheating.
7. When the unit beeps to show that it is preheated, insert the roasting pan in the oven.
8. When the cooking time is complete, remove the roasting pan from the oven and transfer the crab cakes onto serving plates.
9. Serve hot.

Seafood & Tomato Stew

Servings: 8
Preparation Time: 20 minutes
Cooking Time: 4 hours 50 minutes

Ingredients:

- 2 tablespoons olive oil
- 1 pound tomatoes, chopped
- 1 large yellow onion, chopped finely
- 2 garlic cloves, minced
- 2 teaspoons curry powder
- 6 sprigs fresh parsley

- Salt and ground black pepper, as required
- 1½ cups chicken broth
- 1½ pounds salmon, cut into cubes
- 1½ pounds shrimp, peeled and deveined

Instructions:

1. In an oven-safe pan that will fit in the Breville Smart Air Fryer Oven, place all ingredients except for seafood and stir to combine.
2. Cover the pan with a lid.
3. Arrange the pan over the wire rack.
4. Select "Slow Cooker" of Breville Smart Air Fryer Oven and set on "High".
5. Set the timer for 4 hours and press "Start/Stop" to begin cooking.
6. When the cooking time is complete, remove the pan from the oven.
7. Remove the lid and stir in the seafood.
8. Cover the pan with a lid.
9. Again, arrange the pan over the wire rack.
10. Select "Slow Cooker" of Breville Smart Air Fryer Oven and set on "Low".
11. Set the timer for 50 minutes and press "Start/Stop" to begin cooking.
12. When the cooking time is complete, remove the pan from the oven.
13. Remove the lid and stir the mixture well.
14. Serve hot.

Seafood with Pasta

Servings: 4
Preparation Time: 20 minutes
Cooking Time: 18 minutes

Ingredients:

- 14 ounces pasta (of your choice)
- 4 tablespoons pesto, divided
- 4 (4-ounces) salmon steaks
- 2 tablespoons olive oil
- ½ pound cherry tomatoes, chopped
- 8 large prawns, peeled and deveined
- 2 tablespoons fresh lemon juice
- 2 tablespoons fresh thyme, chopped

Instructions:

1. In a large pan of salted boiling water, add the pasta and cook for about 8-10 minutes or until desired doneness.
2. Meanwhile, in the bottom of a baking dish, spread 1 tablespoon of pesto.
3. Place salmon steaks and tomatoes over pesto in a single layer and drizzle with the oil.
4. Arrange the prawns on top in a single layer.
5. Drizzle with lemon juice and sprinkle with thyme.
6. Select "Air Fry" of Breville Smart Air Fryer Oven and adjust the temperature to 390 degrees F.
7. Set the timer for 8 minutes and press "Start/Stop" to begin preheating.
8. When the unit beeps to show that it is preheated, arrange the baking dish over the wire rack.
9. Meanwhile, in a pan of boiling water, cook the pasta for about 10 minutes.
10. Drain the pasta and transfer into a large bowl.
11. When the cooking time is complete, remove the baking dish from oven.
12. Add the remaining pesto and toss to coat well.
13. Divide the pasta onto the serving plate and top with salmon mixture.
14. Serve immediately.

Vegetables, Vegetarian & Vegan Recipes

Green Beans with Carrots

Servings: 3
Preparation Time: 15 minutes
Cooking Time: 10 minutes

Ingredients:

- ½ pound green beans, trimmed
- ½ pound carrots, peeled and cut into sticks
- 1 tablespoon olive oil
- Salt and ground black pepper, as required

Instructions:

1. In a bowl, add all the ingredients and toss to coat well.
2. Place the vegetables in the rotisserie basket and attach the lid.
3. Select "Air Fry" of Breville Smart Air Fryer Oven and adjust the temperature to 400 degrees F.
4. Arrange the vegetables into the greased air fry basket.
5. Set the timer for 10 minutes and press "Start/Stop" to begin preheating.
6. When the unit beeps to show that it is preheated, insert the air fry basket in the oven.
7. When the cooking time is complete, remove the air fry basket from the oven.
8. Serve hot.

Carrot with Zucchini

Servings: 6
Preparation Time: 15 minutes
Cooking Time: 35 minutes

Ingredients:

- 6 teaspoons butter, melted and divided
- ½ pound carrots, peeled and sliced
- 2 pounds zucchinis, sliced
- 1 tablespoon fresh basil, chopped
- Salt and ground black pepper, as required

Instructions:

1. In a bowl, mix together 2 teaspoons of the butter and carrots.
2. Place the carrots into the air fry basket.
3. Select "Air Fry" of Breville Smart Air Fryer Oven and adjust the temperature to 400 degrees F.
4. Set the timer for 35 minutes and press "Start/Stop" to begin preheating.
5. When the unit beeps to show that it is preheated, insert the air fry basket in the oven.
6. Meanwhile, in a large bowl, mix together the remaining butter, zucchini, basil, salt and black pepper.
7. After 5 minutes of cooking, place the zucchini mixture into the basket with carrots.
8. Toss the vegetable mixture 2-3 times during the coking.
9. When the cooking time is complete, remove the air fry basket from the oven and transfer the vegetable mixture onto serving plates.
10. Serve hot.

Broccoli with Sweet Potatoes

Servings: 4
Preparation Time: 15 minutes
Cooking Time: 20 minutes

Ingredients:

- 2 medium sweet potatoes, peeled and cut in 1-inch cubes
- 1 head broccoli, cut in 1-inch florets
- 2 tablespoons vegetable oil
- Salt and ground black pepper, as required

Instructions:

1. In a large bowl, add all the ingredients and toss to coat well.
2. Arrange the vegetables into the greased air fry basket.
3. Select "Roast" of Breville Smart Air Fryer Oven and adjust the temperature to 415 degrees F.
4. Set the timer for 20 minutes and press "Start/Stop" to begin preheating.
5. When the unit beeps to show that it is preheated, insert the air fry basket in the oven.

6. When the cooking time is complete, remove the air fry basket from the oven and transfer the vegetable mixture onto serving plates.
7. Serve hot.

Peas with Mushrooms

Servings: 4
Preparation Time: 15 minutes
Cooking Time: 15 minutes

Ingredients:

- ½ cup soy sauce
- 4 tablespoons maple syrup
- 4 tablespoons rice vinegar
- 4 garlic cloves, chopped finely
- 2 teaspoons Chinese five-spice powder
- ½ teaspoon ground ginger
- 16 ounces Cremini mushrooms, halved
- ½ cup frozen peas

Instructions:

1. In a bowl, add the soy sauce, maple syrup, vinegar, garlic, five-spice powder, and ground ginger and mix well.
2. Place the mushroom into the prepared baking dish in a single layer.
3. Select "Air Fry" of Breville Smart Air Fryer Oven and adjust the temperature to 350 degrees F.
4. Set the timer for 15 minutes and press "Start/Stop" to begin preheating.
5. When the unit beeps to show that it is preheated, arrange the baking dish over the wire rack.
6. After 8 minutes of cooking, add the peas and vinegar mixture into the baking dish and stir to combine.
7. When the cooking time is complete, remove the baking dish from the oven and transfer the vegetable mixture onto serving plates.
8. Serve hot.

Potato with Bell Peppers

Servings: 4
Preparation Time: 15 minutes
Cooking Time: 25 minutes

Ingredients:

- 2 cups water
- 5 russet potatoes, peeled and cubed
- ½ tablespoon extra-virgin olive oil
- ½ of onion, chopped
- ½ of jalapeño, chopped
- 1 large bell pepper, seeded and chopped
- ¼ teaspoon dried oregano, crushed
- ¼ teaspoon garlic powder
- ¼ teaspoon ground cumin
- ¼ teaspoon red chili powder
- Salt and ground black pepper, as required

Instructions:

1. In a large bowl, add the water and potatoes and set aside for about 30 minutes.
2. Drain well and pat dry with the paper towels.
3. In a bowl, add the potatoes and oil and toss to coat well.
4. Arrange the potato cubes into the greased air fry basket.
5. Select "Air Fry" of Breville Smart Air Fryer Oven and adjust the temperature to 330 degrees F.
6. Set the timer for 5 minutes and press "Start/Stop" to begin preheating.
7. When the unit beeps to show that it is preheated, insert the air fry basket in the oven.
8. When the cooking time is complete, remove the air fry basket from the oven and transfer the potato cubes into a large bowl with remaining ingredients and toss to coat well.
9. Place the veggie mixture onto the greased baking dish and spread in an even layer.
10. Select "Air Fry" of Breville Smart Air Fryer Oven and adjust the temperature to 390 degrees F.
11. Set the timer for 20 minutes and press "Start/Stop" to begin preheating.
12. When the unit beeps to show that it is preheated, arrange the baking dish over the wire rack.
13. When the cooking time is complete, remove the baking dish from the oven and transfer the vegetable mixture onto serving plates.
14. Serve hot.

Buttered Veggies

Servings: 3
Preparation Time: 15 minutes
Cooking Time: 20 minutes

Ingredients:

- 1 cup potatoes, chopped
- 1 cup beets, peeled and chopped
- 1 cup carrots, peeled and chopped
- 2 garlic cloves, minced
- Salt and ground black pepper, as required
- 3 tablespoons olive oil

Instructions:

1. In a bowl, place all ingredients and toss to coat well.
2. Place the veggie mixture into the greased enamel roasting pan.
3. Select "Bake" of Breville Smart Air Fryer Oven and adjust the temperature to 450 degrees F.
4. Set the timer for 20 minutes and press "Start/Stop" to begin preheating.
5. When the unit beeps to show that it is preheated, insert the roasting pan in the oven.
6. Toss the veggie mixture once halfway through.
7. When the cooking time is complete, remove the roasting pan from the oven and transfer the vegetable mixture onto serving plates.
8. Serve hot.

Seasoned Veggies

Servings: 4
Preparation Time: 15 minutes
Cooking Time: 12 minutes

Ingredients:

- 1 cup baby carrots
- 1 cup broccoli florets
- 1 cup cauliflower florets
- 1 tablespoon olive oil
- 1 tablespoon Italian seasoning
- Salt and ground black pepper, as required

Instructions:

1. In a bowl, add all the ingredients and toss to coat well.
2. Place the vegetables in the raised air fry basket.
3. Select "Air Fry" of Breville Smart Air Fryer Oven and adjust the temperature to 380 degrees F.

4. Set the timer for 18 minutes and press "Start/Stop" to begin preheating.
5. When the unit beeps to show that it is preheated, insert the air fry basket in the oven.
6. When the cooking time is complete, remove the air fry basket from the oven and transfer the vegetable mixture onto serving plates.
7. Serve hot.

Honey Glazed Veggies

Servings: 4
Preparation Time: 15 minutes
Cooking Time: 20 minutes

Ingredients:

- 2 ounces cherry tomatoes
- 1 large parsnip, peeled and chopped
- 1 large carrot, peeled and chopped
- 1 large zucchini, chopped
- 1 green bell pepper, seeded and chopped
- 6 tablespoons olive oil, divided
- 3 tablespoons honey
- 1 teaspoon Dijon mustard
- 1 teaspoon mixed dried herbs
- 1 teaspoon garlic paste
- Salt and ground black pepper, as required

Instructions:

1. Place the vegetables into the prepared baking dish and drizzle with 3 tablespoons of oil.
2. Select "Air Fry" of Breville Smart Air Fryer Oven and adjust the temperature to 350 degrees F.
3. Set the timer for 15 minutes and press "Start/Stop" to begin preheating.
4. When the unit beeps to show that it is preheated, arrange the baking dish over the wire rack.
5. Flip the veggies once halfway through.
6. Meanwhile, in a bowl, add the remaining oil, honey, mustard, herbs, garlic, salt, and black pepper and mix well.
7. In the baking dish, add the honey mixture and mix until well combined.
8. Select "Air Fry" of Breville Smart Air Fryer Oven and adjust the temperature to 392 degrees F.
9. Set the timer for 5 minutes and press "Start/Stop" to begin cooking.
10. Flip the veggies once halfway through.

11. When the cooking time is complete, remove the baking dish from the oven.
12. Serve hot.

Parmesan Mixed Veggies

Servings: 5
Preparation Time: 15 minutes
Cooking Time: 18 minutes

Ingredients:

- 1 tablespoon olive oil
- 1 tablespoon garlic, minced
- 1 cup cauliflower florets
- 1 cup broccoli florets
- 1 cup zucchini, sliced
- ½ cup yellow squash, sliced
- ½ cup fresh mushrooms, sliced
- 1 small onion, sliced
- ¼ cup balsamic vinegar
- 1 teaspoon red pepper flakes
- Salt and ground black pepper, as required
- ¼ cup Parmesan cheese, grated

Instructions:

1. In a large bowl, add all the ingredients except for cheese and toss to coat well.
2. Arrange the vegetables into the greased air fry basket.
3. Select "Air Fry" of Breville Smart Air Fryer Oven and adjust the temperature to 400 degrees F.
4. Set the timer for 18 minutes and press "Start/Stop" to begin preheating.
5. When the unit beeps to show that it is preheated, insert the roasting pan in the oven.
6. After 8 minutes of cooking, flip the vegetables.
7. After 16 minutes of cooking, sprinkle the vegetables with cheese evenly.
8. When the cooking time is complete, remove the roasting pan from the oven and transfer the vegetable mixture onto serving plates.
9. Serve hot.

Veggie Ratatouille

Servings: 4
Preparation Time: 15 minutes
Cooking Time: 15 minutes

Ingredients:

- 1 green bell pepper, seeded and chopped
- 1 yellow bell pepper, seeded and chopped
- 1 eggplant, chopped
- 1 zucchini, chopped
- 3 tomatoes, chopped
- 2 small onions, chopped
- 2 garlic cloves, minced
- 2 tablespoons Herbs de Provence
- 1 tablespoon olive oil
- 1 tablespoon balsamic vinegar
- Salt and ground black pepper, as required

Instructions:

1. In a large bowl, add the vegetables, garlic, Herbs de Provence, oil, vinegar, salt, and black pepper and toss to coat well.
2. Transfer vegetable mixture into a greased baking dish.
3. Select "Air Fry" of Breville Smart Air Fryer Oven and adjust the temperature to 355 degrees F.
4. Set the timer for 15 minutes and press "Start/Stop" to begin preheating.
5. When the unit beeps to show that it is preheated, arrange the baking dish over the wire rack.
6. When the cooking time is complete, remove the baking dish from oven and transfer the vegetable mixture onto serving plates.
7. Serve hot.

Potato Gratin

Servings: 4
Preparation Time: 15 minutes
Cooking Time: 20 minutes

Ingredients:

- 2 large potatoes, sliced thinly
- 5½ tablespoons cream
- 2 eggs

- 1 tablespoon plain flour
- ½ cup cheddar cheese, grated

Instructions:

1. Arrange the potato slices into the air fry basket.
2. Select "Air Fry" of Breville Smart Air Fryer Oven and adjust the temperature to 355 degrees F.
3. Set the timer for 10 minutes and press "Start/Stop" to begin preheating.
4. When the unit beeps to show that it is preheated, insert the air fry basket in the oven.
5. Meanwhile, in a bowl, add cream, eggs and flour and mix until a thick sauce forms.
6. When the cooking time is complete, remove the air fry basket from the oven.
7. Divide the potato slices in 4 ramekins evenly and top with the egg mixture evenly, followed by the cheese.
8. Arrange the ramekins into the air fry basket and insert in the oven.
9. Select "Air Fry" of Breville Smart Air Fryer Oven and adjust the temperature to 390 degrees F.
10. Set the timer for 10 minutes and press "Start/Stop" to begin cooking.
11. When the cooking time is complete, remove the air fry basket from the oven and place the ramekins onto a wire rack to cool slightly.
12. Serve warm.

Cauliflower Casserole

Servings: 6
Preparation Time: 15 minutes
Cooking Time: 4 hours

Ingredients:

- 24 ounces frozen cauliflower
- 4 ounces cream cheese, cubed
- 1 cup mozzarella cheese, shredded
- 1 cup cheddar cheese, shredded
- 3 scallions, chopped

Instructions:

1. Grease an oven-safe pan that will fit in the Breville Smart Air Fryer Oven.
2. In the pan, place half of the cauliflower in an even layer.

3. Place half of cream cheese cubes over cauliflower, followed by half of both cheeses.
4. Repeat the layers once.
5. Cover the pan with a lid.
6. Arrange the pan over the wire rack.
7. Select "Slow Cooker" of Breville Smart Air Fryer Oven and set on "Low".
8. Set the timer for 4 hours and press "Start/Stop" to begin cooking.
9. When the cooking time is complete, remove the pan from the oven.
10. Remove the lid and serve hot with the garnishing of stallion.

Green Beans & Mushroom Casserole

Servings: 6
Preparation Time: 15 minutes
Cooking Time: 12 minutes

Ingredients:

- 24 ounces fresh green beans, trimmed
- 2 cups fresh button mushrooms, sliced
- 3 tablespoons olive oil
- 2 tablespoons fresh lemon juice
- 1 teaspoon ground sage
- 1 teaspoon garlic powder
- 1 teaspoon onion powder
- Salt and ground black pepper, as required
- 1/3 cup French fried onions

Instructions:

1. In a bowl, add the green beans, mushrooms, oil, lemon juice, sage, and spices and toss to coat well.
2. Arrange the mushroom mixture into the greased air fry basket.
3. Select "Air Fry" of Breville Smart Air Fryer Oven and adjust the temperature to 400 degrees F.
4. Set the timer for 12 minutes and press "Start/Stop" to begin preheating.
5. When the unit beeps to show that it is preheated, insert the air fry basket in the oven.
6. Shake the mushroom mixture occasionally.
7. When the cooking time is complete, remove the air fry basket from the oven and transfer the mushroom mixture into a serving dish.
8. Top with fried onions and serve.

Broccoli Stuffed Tomatoes

Servings: 2
Preparation Time: 15 minutes
Cooking Time: 15 minutes

Ingredients:

- 2 large tomatoes
- ½ cup broccoli, finely chopped
- ½ cup cheddar cheese, shredded
- 1 tablespoon unsalted butter, melted
- ½ teaspoon dried thyme, crushed

Instructions:

1. Slice the top of each tomato and scoop out pulp and seeds.
2. In a bowl, mix together the chopped broccoli and cheese.
3. Stuff each tomato evenly with broccoli mixture.
4. Arrange tomatoes into the greased air fry basket and drizzle with butter.
5. Select "Air Fry" of Breville Smart Air Fryer Oven and adjust the temperature to 355 degrees F.
6. Set the timer for 15 minutes and press "Start/Stop" to begin preheating.
7. When the unit beeps to show that it is preheated, insert the air fry basket in the oven.
8. When the cooking time is complete, remove the air fry basket from the oven and transfer the tomatoes onto a serving platter.
9. Set aside to cool slightly.
10. Garnish with thyme and serve.

Rice Stuffed Tomatoes

Servings: 6
Preparation Time: 15 minutes
Cooking Time: 22 minutes

Ingredients:

- 6 tomatoes
- 1 teaspoon olive oil
- 1 carrot, peeled and finely chopped
- 1 onion, chopped
- 1 cup frozen peas, thawed
- 1 garlic clove, minced

- 2 cups cold cooked rice
- 1 tablespoon soy sauce

Instructions:

1. Cut the top of each tomato and scoop out pulp and seeds.
2. In a skillet, heat oil over low heat and sauté the carrot, onion, garlic, and peas for about 2 minutes.
3. Stir in the soy sauce and rice and remove from heat.
4. Stuff each tomato with the rice mixture.
5. Arrange tomatoes into the greased air fry basket.
6. Select "Air Fry" of Breville Smart Air Fryer Oven and adjust the temperature to 355 degrees F.
7. Set the timer for 20 minutes and press "Start/Stop" to begin preheating.
8. When the unit beeps to show that it is preheated, insert the air fry basket in the oven.
9. When the cooking time is complete, remove the air fry basket from the oven and transfer the tomatoes onto a serving platter.
10. Set aside to cool slightly before serving.

Veggies Stuffed Bell Peppers

Servings: 6
Preparation Time: 20 minutes
Cooking Time: 25 minutes

Ingredients:

- 6 large bell peppers
- 1 bread roll, finely chopped
- 1 carrot, peeled and finely chopped
- 1 onion, finely chopped
- 1 potato, peeled and finely chopped
- ½ cup fresh peas, shelled
- 2 garlic cloves, minced
- 2 teaspoons fresh parsley, chopped
- Salt and ground black pepper, as required
- 1/3 cup cheddar cheese, grated

Instructions:

1. Remove the tops of each bell pepper and discard the seeds.
2. Chop the bell pepper tops finely.

3. In a bowl, place bell pepper tops, bread loaf, vegetables, garlic, parsley, salt and black pepper and mix well.
4. Stuff each bell pepper with the vegetable mixture.
5. Arrange the bell peppers into the greased air fry basket.
6. Select "Air Fry" of Breville Smart Air Fryer Oven and adjust the temperature to 350 degrees F.
7. Set the timer for 25 minutes and press "Start/Stop" to begin preheating.
8. When the unit beeps to show that it is preheated, insert the air fry basket in the oven.
9. After 20 minutes, sprinkle each bell pepper with cheddar cheese.
10. When the cooking time is complete, remove the air fry basket from the oven and transfer the bell peppers onto serving plates.
11. Serve hot.

Rice & Beans Stuffed Bell Peppers

Servings: 5
Preparation Time: 15 minutes
Cooking Time: 15 minutes

Ingredients:

- ½ small bell pepper, seeded and chopped
- 1 (15-ounce) can diced tomatoes with juice
- 1 (15-ounce) can red kidney beans, rinsed and drained
- 1 cup cooked rice
- 1½ teaspoons Italian seasoning
- 5 large bell peppers, tops removed and seeded
- ½ cup mozzarella cheese, shredded
- 1 tablespoon Parmesan cheese, grated

Instructions:

1. In a bowl, mix well-chopped bell pepper, tomatoes with juice, beans, rice, and Italian seasoning.
2. Stuff each bell pepper evenly with the rice mixture.
3. Arrange bell peppers into the greased air fry basket.
4. Select "Air Fry" of Breville Smart Air Fryer Oven and adjust the temperature to 360 degrees F.
5. Set the timer for 15 minutes and press "Start/Stop" to begin preheating.

6. When the unit beeps to show that it is preheated, insert the air fry basket in the oven.
7. Meanwhile, in a bowl, mix together the mozzarella and Parmesan cheese.
8. After 12 minutes of cooking, top each bell pepper with cheese mixture.
9. When the cooking time is complete, remove the air fry basket from the oven and transfer the bell peppers onto a serving platter.
10. Set aside to cool slightly.
11. Serve warm.

Stuffed Eggplants

Servings: 4
Preparation Time: 20 minutes
Cooking Time: 11 minutes

Ingredients:

- 4 small eggplants, halved lengthwise
- 1 teaspoon fresh lime juice
- 1 teaspoon vegetable oil
- 1 small onion, chopped
- ¼ teaspoon garlic, chopped
- ½ of small tomato, chopped
- Salt and ground black pepper, as required
- 1 tablespoon cottage cheese, chopped
- ¼ of green bell pepper, seeded and chopped
- 1 tablespoon tomato paste
- 1 tablespoon fresh cilantro, chopped

Instructions:

1. Carefully cut a slice from one side of each eggplant lengthwise.
2. With a small spoon, scoop out the flesh from each eggplant, leaving a thick shell.
3. Transfer the eggplant flesh into a bowl.
4. Drizzle the eggplants with lime juice evenly.
5. Arrange the hollowed eggplants into the greased air fry basket.
6. Select "Air Fry" of Breville Smart Air Fryer Oven and adjust the temperature to 320 degrees F.
7. Set the timer for 3 minutes and press "Start/Stop" to begin preheating.
8. When the unit beeps to show that it is preheated, insert the air fry basket in the oven.

9. Meanwhile, in a skillet, heat the oil over medium heat and sauté the onion and garlic for about 2 minutes.
10. Add the eggplant flesh, tomato, salt, and black pepper and sauté for about 2 minutes.
11. Stir in the cheese, bell pepper, tomato paste, and cilantro and cook for about 1 minute.
12. Remove the pan of the veggie mixture from heat.
13. When the cooking time is complete, remove the air fry basket from the oven and arrange the cooked eggplants onto a plate.
14. Stuff each eggplant with the veggie mixture.
15. Close each with its cut part.
16. Again arrange the eggplants shells into the greased air fry basket and insert into the oven.
17. Select "Air Fry" of Breville Smart Air Fryer Oven and adjust the temperature to 320 degrees F.
18. Set the timer for 8 minutes and press "Start/Stop" to begin cooking.
19. When the cooking time is complete, remove the air fry basket from the oven and arrange the cooked eggplants onto serving plates.
20. Serve hot.

Stuffed Zucchini

Servings: 4
Preparation Time: 15 minutes
Cooking Time: 35 minutes

Ingredients:

- 2 zucchinis, cut in half lengthwise
- ½ teaspoon garlic powder
- Salt, as required
- 1 teaspoon olive oil
- 4 ounces fresh mushrooms, chopped
- 4 ounces carrots, peeled and shredded
- 3 ounces onion, chopped
- 4 ounces goat cheese, crumbled
- 12 fresh basil leaves
- ½ teaspoon onion powder

Instructions:

1. Carefully scoop the flesh from the middle of each zucchini half.
2. Season each zucchini half with a little garlic powder and salt.
3. Arrange the zucchini halves into the greased baking dish.

4. Select "Bake" of Breville Smart Air Fryer Oven and adjust the temperature to 450 degrees F.
5. Set the timer for 20 minutes and press "Start/Stop" to begin preheating.
6. When the unit beeps to show that it is preheated, arrange the baking dish over the wire rack.
7. Meanwhile, in a skillet, heat the oil over medium heat and cook the mushrooms, carrots, onions, onion powder and salt and cook for about 5-6 minutes.
8. When the cooking time is complete, remove the baking dish from oven and set aside.
9. Stuff each zucchini half with veggie mixture and top with basil leaves, followed by the cheese.
10. Select "Bake" of Breville Smart Air Fryer Oven and adjust the temperature to 450 degrees F.
11. Set the timer for 15 minutes and press "Start/Stop" to begin preheating.
12. When the unit beeps to show that it is preheated, arrange the baking dish over the wire rack.
13. When the cooking time is complete, remove the baking dish from oven and transfer the zucchini halves onto serving plates.
14. Serve warm.

Stuffed Pumpkin

Servings: 5
Preparation Time: 15 minutes
Cooking Time: 30 minutes

Ingredients:

- 1 sweet potato, peeled and chopped
- 1 parsnip, peeled and chopped
- 1 carrot, peeled and chopped
- ½ cup fresh peas, shelled
- 1 onion, chopped
- 2 garlic cloves, minced
- 1 egg, beaten
- 2 teaspoons mixed dried herbs
- Salt and ground black pepper, as required
- ½ of butternut pumpkin, seeded

Instructions:

1. In a large bowl, mix well vegetables, garlic, egg, herbs, salt, and black pepper.
2. Stuff the pumpkin half with vegetable mixture.
3. Arrange pumpkin half into the greased air fry basket.

4. Select "Air Fry" of Breville Smart Air Fryer Oven and adjust the temperature to 355 degrees F.
5. Set the timer for 30 minutes and press "Start/Stop" to begin preheating.
6. When the unit beeps to show that it is preheated, insert the air fry basket in the oven.
7. When the cooking time is complete, remove the air fry basket from the oven and transfer the pumpkin onto a serving platter.
8. Set aside to cool slightly.
9. Serve warm.

Veggie Kabobs

Servings: 6
Preparation Time: 20 minutes
Cooking Time: 10 minutes

Ingredients:

- ¼ cup carrots, peeled and chopped
- ¼ cup French beans
- ½ cup green peas
- 1 teaspoon ginger
- 3 garlic cloves, peeled
- 3 green chilies
- ¼ cup fresh mint leaves
- ½ cup cottage cheese
- 2 medium boiled potatoes, mashed
- ½ teaspoon five-spice powder
- Salt, as required
- 2 tablespoons cornflour
- Olive oil cooking spray

Instructions:

1. In a food processor, add the carrot, beans, peas, ginger, garlic, mint, cheese and pulse until smooth.
2. Transfer the mixture into a bowl.
3. Add the potato, five-spice powder, salt and cornflour and mix until well combined.
4. Divide the mixture into equal-sized small balls.
5. Press each ball around a skewer in a sausage shape.
6. Spray the skewers with cooking spray.
7. Arrange the skewers into the greased air fry basket.
8. Select "Air Fry" of Breville Smart Air Fryer Oven and adjust the temperature to 390 degrees F.

9. Set the timer for 10 minutes and press "Start/Stop" to begin preheating.
10. When the unit beeps to show that it is preheated, insert the air fry basket in the oven.
11. When the cooking time is complete, remove the air fry basket from the oven and transfer the skewers onto a platter.
12. Serve warm.

Onion Soup

Servings: 6
Preparation Time: 15 minutes
Cooking Time: 5 hours 10 minutes

Ingredients:

- 2 tablespoons olive oil
- 2 medium sweet onions, sliced
- 2 garlic cloves, minced
- ¼ cup low-sodium soy sauce
- 1 teaspoon unsweetened applesauce
- 1 teaspoon dried oregano, crushed
- 1 teaspoon dried basil, crushed
- Ground black pepper, as required
- 5 cups vegetable broth
- ¼ cup Parmesan cheese, grated

Instructions:

1. In an oven-safe pan that will fit in the Breville Smart Air Fryer Oven, heat the oil over medium heat and cook the onion for about 8-9 minutes.
2. Add the garlic and cook for about 1 minute.
3. Remove from the heat and stir in the remaining ingredients except for cheese.
4. Cover the pan with a lid.
5. Arrange the pan over the wire rack.
6. Select "Slow Cooker" of Breville Smart Air Fryer Oven and set on "Low".
7. Set the timer for 5 hours and press "Start/Stop" to begin cooking.
8. When the cooking time is complete, remove the pan from the oven.
9. Remove the lid and stir in the cheese until melted completely.
10. Serve hot.

Vegetarian Loaf

Servings: 6
Preparation Time: 20 minutes
Cooking Time: 1½ hours

Ingredients:

- 1 (14½-ounce) can vegetable broth
- ¾ cup brown lentils, rinsed
- 1 tablespoon olive oil
- 1¾ cups carrots, peeled and shredded
- 1 cup fresh mushrooms, chopped
- 1 cup onion, chopped
- 1 tablespoon fresh parsley, minced
- 1 tablespoon fresh basil, minced
- ½ cup cooked brown rice
- 1 cup mozzarella cheese, shredded
- 1 large egg
- 1 large egg white
- Salt and ground black pepper, as required
- 2 tablespoons tomato paste
- 2 tablespoons water

Instructions:

1. In a pan, place the broth over medium-high heat and bring to a boil.
2. Stir in the lentils and again bring to a boil.
3. Reduce the heat to low and simmer, covered for about 30 minutes.
4. Remove from the heat and set aside to cool slightly.
5. Meanwhile, in a large skillet, heat the oil over medium heat and sauté the carrots, mushrooms and onion for about 10 minutes.
6. Stir in herbs and remove from the heat.
7. Transfer the veggie mixture into a large bowl and set aside to cool slightly.
8. After cooling, add the lentils, rice, cheese, egg, egg white and seasonings and lentils and mix until well combined.
9. In a small bowl, stir together the tomato paste and water.
10. Place the mixture into a greased parchment paper-lined loaf pan and top with water mixture.
11. Select "Bake" of Breville Smart Air Fryer Oven and adjust the temperature to 350 degrees F.
12. Set the timer for 50 minutes and press "Start/Stop" to begin preheating.

13. When the unit beeps to show that it is preheated, arrange the loaf pan over the wire rack.
14. When the cooking time is complete, remove the loaf pan from oven and place onto a wire rack for about 10 minutes before slicing.
15. Carefully invert the loaf onto the wire rack.
16. Cut into desired sized slices and serve.

Pita Bread Pizza

Servings: 1
Preparation Time: 10 minutes
Cooking Time: 5 minutes

Ingredients:

- 2 tablespoons marinara sauce
- 1 whole-wheat pita bread
- ½ cup fresh baby spinach leaves
- ½ of small plum tomato, cut into 4 slices
- ½ of garlic clove, sliced thinly
- ½ ounce part-skim mozzarella cheese, shredded
- ½ tablespoon Parmigiano-Reggiano cheese, shredded

Instructions:

1. Arrange the pita bread onto a plate.
2. Spread marinara sauce over 1 side of each pita bread evenly.
3. Top with the spinach leaves, followed by tomato slices, garlic and cheeses.
4. Arrange the pita bread into the greased air fry basket.
5. Select "Air Fry" of Breville Smart Air Fryer Oven and adjust the temperature to 350 degrees F.
6. Set the timer for 5 minutes and press "Start/Stop" to begin preheating.
7. When the unit beeps to show that it is preheated, insert the air fry basket in the oven.
8. When the cooking time is complete, remove the air fry basket from the oven and transfer the pizza onto a serving plate.
9. Set aside to cool slightly.
10. Serve warm.

Tofu In Orange Sauce

Servings: 4
Preparation Time: 15 minutes
Cooking Time: 10 minutes

Ingredients:

For Tofu:

- 1-pound extra-firm tofu, pressed and cubed
- 1 tablespoon cornstarch
- 1 tablespoon tamari

For Sauce:

- ½ cup water
- 1/3 cup fresh orange juice
- 1 tablespoon maple syrup
- 1 teaspoon orange zest, grated
- 1 teaspoon garlic, minced
- 1 teaspoon fresh ginger, minced
- 2 teaspoons cornstarch
- ¼ teaspoon red pepper flakes, crushed
- Ground black pepper, as required

Instructions:

1. In a bowl, add the tofu, cornstarch, and tamari and toss to coat well.
2. Set the tofu aside to marinate for at least 15 minutes.
3. Arrange the tofu cubes into the greased basket.
4. Select "Air Fry" of Breville Smart Air Fryer Oven and adjust the temperature to 390 degrees F.
5. Set the timer for 10 minutes and press "Start/Stop" to begin preheating.
6. When the unit beeps to show that it is preheated, insert the air fry basket in the oven.
7. Flip the tofu cubes once halfway through.
8. Meanwhile, for the sauce: in a small pan, add all the ingredients over medium-high heat and bring to a boil, stirring continuously.
9. When the cooking time is complete, remove the air fry basket from the oven.
10. Transfer the tofu into a serving bowl with the sauce and gently stir to combine.
11. Serve immediately.

Tofu In Sweet & Sour Sauce

Servings: 4
Preparation Time: 20 minutes
Cooking Time: 20 minutes

Ingredients:

For Tofu:

- 1 (14-ounce) block firm tofu, pressed and cubed
- ½ cup arrowroot flour
- ½ teaspoon sesame oil

For Sauce:

- 4 tablespoons low-sodium soy sauce
- 1½ tablespoons rice vinegar
- 1½ tablespoons chili sauce
- 1 tablespoon agave nectar
- 2 large garlic cloves, minced
- 1 teaspoon fresh ginger, peeled and grated
- 2 scallions (green part), chopped

Instructions:

1. In a bowl, mix together the tofu, arrowroot flour, and sesame oil.
2. Arrange the tofu cubes into the greased air fry basket.
3. Select "Air Fry" of Breville Smart Air Fryer Oven and adjust the temperature to 360 degrees F.
4. Set the timer for 20 minutes and press "Start/Stop" to begin preheating.
5. When the unit beeps to show that it is preheated, insert the air fry basket in the oven.
6. Flip the tofu cubes once halfway through.
7. Meanwhile, for the sauce: in a bowl, add all the ingredients except scallions and beat until well combined.
8. When the cooking time is complete, remove the air fry basket from the oven.
9. Transfer the tofu into a skillet with sauce over medium heat and cook for about 3 minutes, stirring occasionally.
10. Garnish with scallions and serve hot.

Tofu with Peanut Butter Sauce

Servings: 3
Preparation Time: 20 minutes
Cooking Time: 15 minutes

Ingredients:

For Tofu:

- 2 tablespoons fresh lime juice
- 2 tablespoons soy sauce
- 1 tablespoon maple syrup
- 1 teaspoon Sriracha sauce
- 2 teaspoons fresh ginger, peeled
- 2 garlic cloves, peeled
- 1 (14-ounces) block tofu, pressed and cut into strips

For Sauce:

- 1 (2-inch) piece fresh ginger, peeled
- 2 garlic cloves, peeled
- ½ cup creamy peanut butter
- 1 tablespoon soy sauce
- 1 tablespoon fresh lime juice
- 1-2 teaspoons Sriracha sauce
- 6 tablespoons water

Instructions:

1. For tofu: in a food processor, put all the ingredients except tofu and pulse until smooth.
2. In a bowl, mix together the marinade and tofu.
3. Set aside to marinate for about 20-30 minutes.
4. Meanwhile, soak 6 bamboo skewers into the water for about 30 minutes.
5. With a cutter, cut each skewer in half.
6. Thread one tofu strip onto each little bamboo stick.
7. Arrange tofu skewers into the greased air fry basket in a single layer.
8. Select "Air Fry" of Breville Smart Air Fryer Oven and adjust the temperature to 370 degrees F.
9. Set the timer for 15 minutes and press "Start/Stop" to begin preheating.
10. When the unit beeps to show that it is preheated, insert the air fry basket in the oven.

11. For the sauce: add all the ingredients in a food processor and pulse until smooth.
12. When the cooking time is complete, remove the air fry basket from the oven and transfer the tofu cubes onto serving plates.
13. Top with the sauce and serve.

Tofu with Capers Sauce

Servings: 4
Preparation Time: 20 minutes
Cooking Time: 20 minutes

Ingredients:

For Marinade:

- ¼ cup fresh lemon juice
- 2 tablespoons fresh parsley
- 1 garlic clove, peeled
- Salt and ground black pepper, as required

For Tofu:

- 1 (14-ounce) block extra-firm tofu, pressed and cut into 8 rectangular cutlets
- ½ cup mayonnaise
- 1 cup panko breadcrumbs

For Sauce:

- 1 cup vegetable broth
- ¼ cup lemon juice
- 1 garlic clove, peeled
- 2 tablespoons fresh parsley
- 2 teaspoons cornstarch
- Salt and ground black pepper, as required
- 2 tablespoons capers

Instructions:

1. For marinade: in a food processor, add all the ingredients and pulse until smooth.
2. In a bowl, mix together the marinade and tofu.
3. Set aside for about 15-30 minutes.
4. In 2 shallow bowls, place the mayonnaise and panko breadcrumbs, respectively.
5. Coat the tofu pieces with mayonnaise and then roll into the panko.

6. Arrange the tofu cubes into the greased air fry basket.
7. Select "Air Fry" of Breville Smart Air Fryer Oven and adjust the temperature to 375 degrees F.
8. Set the timer for 20 minutes and press "Start/Stop" to begin preheating.
9. When the unit beeps to show that it is preheated, insert the air fry basket in the oven.
10. Flip the tofu cubes once halfway through.
11. Meanwhile, for the sauce: add broth, lemon juice, garlic, parsley, cornstarch, salt and black pepper in a food processor and pulse until smooth.
12. Transfer the sauce into a small pan and stir in the capers.
13. Place the pan over medium heat and bring to a boil.
14. Reduce the heat to low and simmer for about 5-7 minutes, stirring continuously.
15. When the cooking time is complete, remove the air fry basket from the oven and transfer the tofu cubes onto serving plates.
16. Top with the sauce and serve.

Tofu with Cauliflower

Servings: 2
Preparation Time: 15 minutes
Cooking Time: 16 minutes

Ingredients

- ½ (14-ounce) block firm tofu, pressed and cubed
- ½ small head cauliflower, cut into florets
- 1 tablespoon canola oil
- 1 tablespoon nutritional yeast
- ¼ teaspoon dried parsley
- 1 teaspoon ground turmeric
- ¼ teaspoon paprika
- Salt and ground black pepper, as required

Instructions:

1. In a bowl, mix together all the ingredients.
2. Place the tofu mixture in the greased enamel roasting pan.
3. Select "Air Fry" of Breville Smart Air Fryer Oven and adjust the temperature to 390 degrees F.
4. Set the timer for 16 minutes and press "Start/Stop" to begin preheating.
5. When the unit beeps to show that it is preheated, insert the roasting pan in the oven.

6. Toss the tofu mixture once halfway through.
7. When the cooking time is complete, remove the baking dish from the oven and transfer the tofu mixture onto serving plates.
8. Serve hot.

Tofu with Broccoli

Servings: 3
Preparation Time: 15 minutes
Cooking Time: 15 minutes

Ingredients:

- 8 ounces firm tofu, drained, pressed and cubed
- 1 head broccoli, cut into florets
- 1 tablespoon butter, melted
- 1 teaspoon ground turmeric
- ¼ teaspoon paprika
- Salt and ground black pepper, as required

Instructions:

1. In a bowl, mix together all ingredients.
2. Place the tofu mixture in the greased baking dish.
3. Select "Air Fry" of Breville Smart Air Fryer Oven and adjust the temperature to 390 degrees F.
4. Set the timer for 15 minutes and press "Start/Stop" to begin preheating.
5. When the unit beeps to show that it is preheated, insert the baking dish in the oven.
6. Toss the tofu mixture once halfway through.
7. When the cooking time is complete, remove the baking dish from the oven and transfer the tofu mixture onto serving plates.
8. Serve hot.

Tofu with Veggies

Servings: 3
Preparation Time: 20 minutes
Cooking Time: 22 minutes

Ingredients:

- ½ (14-ounces) block firm tofu, pressed and crumbled
- 1 cup carrot, peeled and chopped
- ½ cup onion, chopped
- 4 tablespoons low-sodium soy sauce, divided

- 1 teaspoon ground turmeric
- 3 cups cauliflower rice
- ½ cup broccoli, finely chopped
- ½ cup frozen peas
- 1 tablespoon fresh ginger, minced
- 2 garlic cloves, minced
- 1 tablespoon rice vinegar
- 1½ teaspoons sesame oil, toasted

Instructions:

1. In a bowl, mix together the tofu, carrot, onion, 2 tablespoons of soy sauce, and turmeric.
2. Arrange tofu mixture into the greased baking dish.
3. Select "Air Fry" of Breville Smart Air Fryer Oven and adjust the temperature to 370 degrees F.
4. Set the timer for 22 minutes and press "Start/Stop" to begin preheating.
5. When the unit beeps to show that it is preheated, insert the baking dish in the oven.
6. Meanwhile, in a large bowl, mix together the cauliflower rice, broccoli, peas, ginger, garlic, vinegar, sesame oil, and remaining soy sauce.
7. After 10 minutes of cooking, stir the vegetable mixture into the baking dish.
8. Shake the baking dish once halfway through.
9. When the cooking time is complete, remove the baking dish from the oven and transfer the tofu mixture onto serving plates.
10. Serve hot.

Mixed Veggies Soup

Servings: 6
Preparation Time: 15 minutes
Cooking Time: 8 hours 5 minutes

Ingredients:

- 1 tablespoon olive oil
- 1 yellow onion, chopped
- 1 celery stalk, chopped
- 1 large carrot, peeled and chopped
- 2 garlic cloves, minced
- 1 teaspoon dried oregano, crushed
- 1 large zucchini, chopped
- 2 tomatoes, chopped
- 1 cup fresh spinach, chopped
- 4 cups homemade vegetable broth

- Salt and ground black pepper, as required

Instructions:

1. In an oven-safe pan that will fit in the Breville Smart Air Fryer Oven, heat the oil over medium heat and sauté the onion, celery and carrot for about 3-4 minutes.
2. Add the garlic and thyme and sauté for about 1 minute.
3. Remove from the heat and stir in the remaining ingredients.
4. Cover the pan with a lid.
5. Arrange the pan over the wire rack.
6. Select "Slow Cooker" of Breville Smart Air Fryer Oven and set on "Low".
7. Set the timer for 8 hours and press "Start/Stop" to begin cooking.
8. When the cooking time is complete, remove the pan from the oven.
9. Remove the lid and stir the mixture well.
10. Serve hot.

Lentil & Veggie Soup

Servings: 12
Preparation Time: 20 minutes
Cooking Time: 9 hours 10 minutes

Ingredients:

- 2 tablespoons olive oil
- 3 cups onions, chopped finely
- 3 cups celery stalk, chopped finely
- 4 garlic cloves, minced
- 1 teaspoon ground coriander
- 1 teaspoon ground cumin
- 1 teaspoon ground turmeric
- ¼ teaspoon ground cinnamon
- Ground black pepper, as required
- 3 cups cauliflower, chopped
- 1 (28-ounce) can diced tomatoes
- 1¾ cups lentils
- 2 tablespoons tomato paste
- 6 cups vegetable broth
- 2 cups water
- 4 cups fresh spinach, chopped
- ½ cup fresh cilantro, chopped

Instructions:

1. In an oven-safe pan that will fit in the Breville Smart Air Fryer Oven, heat the oil over medium heat and cook the onion and celery for about 8-9 minutes, stirring frequently.
2. Add the garlic and spices and cook for about 1 minute.
3. Remove from the heat and stir in the remaining ingredients except for spinach and cilantro.
4. Cover the pan with a lid.
5. Arrange the pan over the wire rack.
6. Select "Slow Cooker" of Breville Smart Air Fryer Oven and set on "Low".
7. Set the timer for 9 hours and press "Start/Stop" to begin cooking.
8. In the last 30 minutes of cooking, stir in the spinach.
9. When the cooking time is complete, remove the pan from the oven.
10. Remove the lid and serve hot with the garnishing of cilantro.

Beans & Quinoa Chili

Servings: 6
Preparation Time: 15 minutes
Cooking Time: 6 hours 10 minutes

Ingredients:

- 2 teaspoons olive oil
- 1 large yellow onion, chopped
- 2 celery stalks, chopped
- 3 garlic cloves, chopped
- ¼ cup water
- 2 tablespoons tomato paste
- 1½ tablespoons chipotle in adobo, chopped finely
- 2 teaspoons chili powder
- 1 teaspoon ground coriander
- 1 teaspoon ground cumin
- ½ teaspoon ground cinnamon
- ½ teaspoon smoked paprika
- Pinch of cayenne pepper
- 3 cups vegetable broth
- 3 cups cooked black beans
- 1 cup uncooked quinoa, rinsed
- 1-1¼ pounds butternut squash, peeled and cubed

- 1 (15-ounce) can fire-roasted, diced tomatoes with juice
- 1 small avocado, peeled, pitted and sliced

Instructions:

1. In an oven-safe pan that will fit in the Breville Smart Air Fryer Oven, heat the oil over medium heat and cook the onion and celery for about 5-7 minutes, stirring frequently.
2. Add the garlic and cook for about 1 minute, stirring continuously.
3. Add the water, tomato paste, chipotle and spices and cook for about 1 minute, stirring continuously.
4. Remove from the heat and stir in the broth, black beans, quinoa, squash and tomatoes with juice.
5. Cover the pan with a lid.
6. Arrange the pan over the wire rack.
7. Select "Slow Cooker" of Breville Smart Air Fryer Oven and set on "Low".
8. Set the timer for 6 hours and press "Start/Stop" to begin cooking.
9. When the cooking time is complete, remove the pan from the oven.
10. Remove the lid and stir the mixture well.
11. Serve hot with the topping of avocado slices.

Beans with Veggies

Servings: 6
Preparation Time: 15 minutes
Cooking Time: 4 hours

Ingredients:

- 2 (15-ounce) cans cannellini beans, rinsed and drained
- 1 (14½-ounce) can diced tomatoes with basil, garlic and oregano
- 1 cup zucchini, chopped
- 1 cup red bell pepper, seeded and chopped
- ½ cup Kalamata olives, pitted and halved
- 2 garlic cloves, minced
- ¼ cup fresh parsley, chopped
- Salt and ground black pepper, as required
- 2 tablespoons balsamic vinegar
- 2 tablespoons fresh lemon juice
- 1 cup vegetable broth
- ¼ cup feta cheese, crumbled

Instructions:

1. In an oven-safe pan that will fit in the Breville Smart Air Fryer Oven, place all ingredients and stir to combine.
2. Cover the pan with a lid.
3. Arrange the pan over the wire rack.
4. Select "Slow Cooker" of Breville Smart Air Fryer Oven and set on "Low".
5. Set the timer for 4 hours and press "Start/Stop" to begin cooking.
6. When the cooking time is complete, remove the pan from the oven.
7. Remove the lid and serve hot with the topping of feta cheese.

Beans with Veggies

Servings: 6
Preparation Time: 15 minutes
Cooking Time: 4 hours

Ingredients:

- 2 (15-ounce) cans cannellini beans, rinsed and drained
- 1 (14½-ounce) can diced tomatoes with basil, garlic and oregano
- 1 cup zucchini, chopped
- 1 cup red bell pepper, seeded and chopped
- ½ cup Kalamata olives, pitted and halved
- 2 garlic cloves, minced
- ¼ cup fresh parsley, chopped
- Freshly ground black pepper, to taste
- 2 tablespoons balsamic vinegar
- 2 tablespoons fresh lemon juice
- 1 cup vegetable broth
- ¼ cup feta cheese, crumbled

Instructions:

1. In an oven-safe pan that will fit in the Breville Smart Air Fryer Oven, place all ingredients except for feta cheese and stir to combine.
2. Cover the pan with a lid.
3. Arrange the pan over the wire rack.
4. Select "Slow Cooker" of Breville Smart Air Fryer Oven and set on "Low".
5. Set the timer for 5 hours and press "Start/Stop" to begin cooking.

6. When the cooking time is complete, remove the pan from the oven.
7. Remove the lid and stir the mixture well.
8. Serve hot with the topping of feta cheese.

Beans & Veggie Burgers

Servings: 4
Preparation Time: 20 minutes
Cooking Time: 22 minutes

Ingredients:

- 1 cup cooked black beans
- 2 cups boiled potatoes, peeled and mashed
- 1 cup fresh spinach, chopped
- 1 cup fresh mushrooms, chopped
- 2 teaspoons Chile lime seasoning
- Olive oil cooking spray

Instructions:

1. In a large bowl, add the beans, potatoes, spinach, mushrooms, and seasoning and with your hands, mix until well combined.
2. Make 4 equal-sized patties from the mixture.
3. Spray the patties with cooking spray evenly.
4. Arrange the patties into the greased air fry basket.
5. Select "Air Fry" of Breville Smart Air Fryer Oven and adjust the temperature to 370 degrees F.
6. Set the timer for 22 minutes and press "Start/Stop" to begin preheating.
7. When the unit beeps to show that it is preheated, insert the air fry basket in the oven.
8. Flip the patties once after 12 minutes.
9. When the cooking time is complete, remove the air fry basket from the oven.
10. Serve hot.

Veggies Rice

Servings: 4
Preparation Time: 15 minutes
Cooking Time: 18 minutes

Ingredients:

- 2 cups cooked white rice
- 1 tablespoon vegetable oil

- 2 teaspoons sesame oil, toasted and divided
- 1 tablespoon water
- Salt and ground white pepper, as required
- 1 large egg, lightly beaten
- ½ cup frozen peas, thawed
- ½ cup frozen carrots, thawed
- 1 teaspoon soy sauce
- 1 teaspoon Sriracha sauce
- ½ teaspoon sesame seeds, toasted

Instructions:

1. In a large bowl, add the rice, vegetable oil, one teaspoon of sesame oil, water, salt, and white pepper and mix well.
2. Place the rice mixture into the greased baking dish.
3. Select "Air Fry" of Breville Smart Air Fryer Oven and adjust the temperature to 380 degrees F.
4. Set the timer for 18 minutes and press "Start/Stop" to begin preheating.
5. When the unit beeps to show that it is preheated, arrange the baking dish over the wire rack.
6. Stir the rice mixture once halfway through.
7. After 12 minutes of cooking, place the beaten egg over rice.
8. After 15 minutes of cooking, stir in the peas and carrots.
9. Meanwhile, in a bowl, mix together soy sauce, Sriracha sauce, sesame seeds and the remaining sesame oil.
10. When the cooking time is complete, remove the baking dish from oven and transfer the rice mixture into a serving bowl.
11. Drizzle with the sauce and serve.

Mac n' Cheese

Servings: 4
Preparation Time: 10 minutes
Cooking Time: 25 minutes

Ingredients:

- 2 cups cheddar cheese, shredded and divided
- 1 teaspoon cornstarch
- 2 cup heavy whipping cream
- 2 cups dry macaroni

Instructions:

1. In a bowl, place 1½ cups of cheese and cornstarch and mix well. Set aside.
2. In another bowl, place the remaining cheese, whipping cream and macaroni and mix well.
3. Transfer the macaroni mixture into a baking dish that will fit in the Vortex Plus Air Fryer Oven.
4. With a piece of foil, cover the baking dish.
5. Select "Air Fry" of Breville Smart Air Fryer Oven and adjust the temperature to 310 degrees F.
6. Set the timer for 25 minutes and press "Start/Stop" to begin preheating.
7. When the unit beeps to show that it is preheated, arrange the baking dish over the wire rack.
8. After 15 minutes, remove the foil and top the macaroni mixture with cornstarch mixture.
9. When the cooking time is complete, remove the baking dish from oven and set aside to cool slightly.
10. Serve warm.

Dessert Recipes

Pineapple Bites

Servings: 4
Preparation Time: 10 minutes
Cooking Time: 10 minutes

Ingredients:

For Pineapple Sticks:

- ½ of pineapple
- ¼ cup desiccated coconut

For Yogurt Dip:

- 1 tablespoon fresh mint leaves, minced
- 1 cup vanilla yogurt

Instructions:

1. Remove the outer skin of the pineapple and cut into long 1-2-inch-thick sticks.
2. In a shallow dish, place the coconut.
3. Coat the pineapple sticks with coconut evenly.
4. Arrange the pineapple sticks into the lightly greased air fry basket.
5. Select "Air Fry" of Breville Smart Air Fryer Oven and adjust the temperature to 390 degrees F.
6. Set the timer for 10 minutes and press "Start/Stop" to begin preheating.
7. When the unit beeps to show that it is preheated, insert the air fry basket in the oven.
8. Meanwhile, for dip: in a bowl, mix together mint and yogurt.
9. When the cooking time is complete, remove the air fry basket from the oven and transfer the pineapple slices onto a serving plate.
10. Serve pineapple sticks with yogurt dip.

Glazed Figs

Servings: 4
Preparation Time: 10 minutes
Cooking Time: 10 minutes

Ingredients:

- 4 fresh figs
- 4 teaspoons honey
- 2/3 cup Mascarpone cheese, softened
- Pinch of ground cinnamon

Instructions:

1. Cut each fig into the quarter, leaving just a little at the base to hold the fruit together.
2. Arrange the figs onto parchment paper-lined enamel roasting pan and drizzle with honey.
3. Place about 2 teaspoons of Mascarpone cheese in the center of each fig and sprinkle with cinnamon.
4. Arrange the figs into the enamel roasting pan.
5. Select "Broil" of Breville Smart Air Fryer Oven and set the timer for 15 minutes. and press "Start/Stop" to begin preheating.
6. When the unit beeps to show that it is preheated, insert the roasting pan in the oven.
7. When the cooking time is complete, remove the roasting pan from the oven and transfer the figs onto serving plates.
8. Serve warm.

Glazed Banana

Servings: 4
Preparation Time: 10 minutes
Cooking Time: 10 minutes

Ingredients:

- 2 ripe bananas, peeled and sliced lengthwise
- 1 teaspoon fresh lime juice
- 4 teaspoons maple syrup
- 1/8 teaspoon ground cinnamon

Instructions:

1. Coat each banana half with lime juice.
2. Arrange the banana halves onto the greased baking dish, cut sides up.
3. Drizzle the banana halves with maple syrup and sprinkle with cinnamon.
4. Select "Air Fry" of Breville Smart Air Fryer Oven and adjust the temperature to 350 degrees F.
5. Set the timer for 10 minutes and press "Start/Stop" to begin preheating.

6. When the unit beeps to show that it is preheated, arrange the baking dish over the wire rack.
7. When the cooking time is complete, remove the baking dish from the oven.
8. Serve immediately.

Banana Split

Servings: 8
Preparation Time: 15 minutes
Cooking Time: 14 minutes

Ingredients:

- 3 tablespoons coconut oil
- 1 cup panko breadcrumbs
- ½ cup cornflour
- 2 eggs
- 4 bananas, peeled and halved lengthwise
- 3 tablespoons sugar
- ¼ teaspoon ground cinnamon
- 2 tablespoons walnuts, chopped

Instructions:

1. In a medium skillet, melt the coconut oil over medium heat and cook breadcrumbs for about 3-4 minutes or until golden browned and crumbled, stirring continuously.
2. Transfer the breadcrumbs into a shallow bowl and set aside to cool.
3. In a second bowl, place the cornflour.
4. In a third bowl, whisk the eggs.
5. Coat the banana slices with flour and then dip into eggs and, finally, coat evenly with the breadcrumbs.
6. In a small bowl, mix together the sugar and cinnamon.
7. Arrange the banana slices into the air fry basket and sprinkle with cinnamon sugar.
8. Select "Air Fry" of Breville Smart Air Fryer Oven and adjust the temperature to 280 degrees F.
9. Set the timer for 10 minutes and press "Start/Stop" to begin preheating.
10. When the unit beeps to show that it is preheated, insert the air fry basket in the oven.
11. When the cooking time is complete, remove the air fry basket from the oven and transfer the banana slices onto plates to cool slightly
12. Sprinkle with chopped walnuts and serve.

Sugared Grapefruit

Servings: 2
Preparation Time: 5 minutes
Cooking Time: 10 minutes

Ingredients:

- 2 tablespoons granulated sugar
- 2 teaspoons brown sugar
- 1 large grapefruit, halved
- Pinch of flaky sea salt

Instructions:

1. In a small bowl, mix together both sugars.
2. Arrange the grapefruit halves onto the greased enamel roasting pan, cut sides up and sprinkle with sugar mixture.
3. Select "Broil" of Breville Smart Air Fryer Oven and set the timer for 5 minutes.
4. Press "Start/Stop" to begin preheating.
5. When the unit beeps to show that it is preheated, insert the roasting pan in the oven.
6. When the cooking time is complete, remove the roasting pan from the oven and place the grapefruit halves onto serving plates.
7. Sprinkle with sea salt and serve.

Nutty Pears

Servings: 2
Preparation Time: 10 minutes
Cooking Time: 30 minutes

Ingredients:

- 1 ripe Anjou pear, halved and cored
- 1/8 teaspoon ground cinnamon
- 6 semisweet chocolate chips
- 2 tablespoons pecans, chopped
- 1 teaspoon pure maple syrup

Instructions:

1. Arrange the pear halves onto the greased enamel roasting pan, cut sides up and sprinkle with cinnamon.
2. Top each half with chocolate chips and pecans and drizzle with maple syrup.
3. Arrange the pears into the greased enamel roasting pan.
4. Select "Air Fry" of Breville Smart Air Fryer Oven and adjust the temperature to 350 degrees F.
5. Set the timer for 30 minutes and press "Start/Stop" to begin preheating.
6. When the unit beeps to show that it is preheated, insert the roasting pan in the oven.
7. When the cooking time is complete, remove the roasting pan from the oven and set aside to cool slightly.
8. Serve warm.

Shortbread Fingers

Servings: 10
Preparation Time: 15 minutes
Cooking Time: 12 minutes

Ingredients:

- 1/3 cup caster sugar
- 1 2/3 cups plain flour
- ¾ cup butter

Instructions:

1. In a large bowl, mix together the sugar and flour.
2. Add the butter and mix until a smooth dough forms.
3. Cut the dough into 10 equal-sized fingers.
4. With a fork, lightly prick the fingers.
5. Place the fingers into the lightly greased baking dish.
6. Select "Air Fry" of Breville Smart Air Fryer Oven and adjust the temperature to 355 degrees F.
7. Set the timer for 12 minutes and press "Start/Stop" to begin preheating.
8. When the unit beeps to show that it is preheated, arrange the baking dish over the wire rack.
9. When the cooking time is complete, remove the baking dish from oven and place onto a wire rack to cool for about 5-10 minutes.
10. Now, invert the shortbread fingers onto the wire rack to completely cool before serving.

Marshmallow Pastries

Servings: 4
Preparation Time: 10 minutes
Cooking Time: 15 minutes

Ingredients:

- 4 phyllo pastry sheets, thawed
- 2 ounces butter, melted
- ¼ cup chunky peanut butter
- 4 teaspoons marshmallow fluff
- Pinch of salt

Instructions:

1. Brush 1 sheet of phyllo with butter.
2. Place the second sheet of phyllo on top of the first one and brush it with butter.
3. Repeat until all 4 sheets are used.
4. Cut the phyllo layers in 4 (3x12-inch) strips.
5. Place 1 tablespoon of peanut butter and 1 teaspoon of marshmallow fluff on the underside of a strip of phyllo.
6. Carefully fold the tip of the sheet over the filling to make a triangle.
7. Fold repeatedly in a zigzag manner until the filling is fully covered.
8. Arrange the pastries into the greased air fry basket and insert in the oven.
9. Select "Air Fry" of Breville Smart Air Fryer Oven and adjust the temperature to 360 degrees F.
10. Set the timer for 15 minutes and press "Start/Stop" to begin preheating.
11. When the unit beeps to show that it is preheated, insert the air fry basket in the oven.
12. When the cooking time is complete, remove the air fry basket from the oven and set aside to cool slightly.
13. Sprinkle with a pinch of salt and serve warm.

Apple Pastries

Servings: 6
Preparation Time: 15 minutes
Cooking Time: 0 minutes

Ingredients:

- ½ of large apple, peeled, cored and chopped

- 1 teaspoon fresh orange zest, grated finely
- ½ tablespoon white sugar
- ½ teaspoon ground cinnamon
- 7.05 ounces prepared frozen puff pastry

Instructions:

1. In a bowl, mix together all ingredients except puff pastry.
2. Cut the pastry in 16 squares.
3. Place about a teaspoon of the apple mixture in the center of each square.
4. Fold each square into a triangle and press the edges slightly with wet fingers.
5. Then with a fork, press the edges firmly.
6. Arrange the pastries into the greased air fry basket and insert in the oven.
7. Select "Air Fry" of Breville Smart Air Fryer Oven and adjust the temperature to 390 degrees F.
8. Set the timer for 10 minutes and press "Start/Stop" to begin preheating.
9. When the unit beeps to show that it is preheated, insert the air fry basket in the oven.
10. When the cooking time is complete, remove the air fry basket from the oven and set aside to cool slightly.
11. Serve warm.

Chocolate Pastries

Servings: 4
Preparation Time: 20 minutes
Cooking Time: 10 minutes

Ingredients:

- 8 ounces frozen puff pastry, thawed
- 4 tablespoons hazelnut spread
- 4 teaspoons slivered almonds plus more for topping
- 1 egg, beaten
- 1 tablespoon water
- 2 tablespoons turbinado sugar

Instructions:

1. Place the puff pastry onto a lightly floured surface and unfold it.
2. Cut the pastry into 4 squares.

3. Place 1 tablespoon of hazelnut spread on each square and top with almonds.
4. With wet fingers, moisten the edges of each pastry and fold into a rectangle shape.
5. With a fork, press the edges to seal.
6. In a small bowl, add the egg and 1 tablespoon of water and beat well.
7. Coat the top of each pastry with the egg wash and sprinkle with turbinado sugar, followed by a few slivered almonds.
8. Arrange the pastries into the enamel roasting pan.
9. Select "Air Fry" of Breville Smart Air Fryer Oven and adjust the temperature to 330 degrees F.
10. Set the timer for 10 minutes and press "Start/Stop" to begin preheating.
11. When the unit beeps to show that it is preheated, insert the roasting pan in the oven.
12. When the cooking time is complete, remove the roasting pan from the oven and set aside to cool slightly.
13. Serve warm.

Walnut Brownies

Servings: 4
Preparation Time: 15 minutes
Cooking Time: 22 minutes

Ingredients:

- ½ cup chocolate, roughly chopped
- 1/3 cup butter
- 5 tablespoons sugar
- 1 egg, beaten
- 1 teaspoon vanilla extract
- Pinch of salt
- 5 tablespoons self-rising flour
- ¼ cup walnuts, chopped

Instructions:

1. In a microwave-safe bowl, add the chocolate and butter. Microwave on high heat for about 2 minutes, stirring after every 30 seconds.
2. Remove from microwave and set aside to cool.
3. In another bowl, add the sugar, egg, vanilla extract and salt and whisk until creamy and light.
4. Add the chocolate mixture and whisk until well combined.
5. Add the flour and walnuts and mix until well combined.

6. Line a baking dish with a greased parchment paper.
7. Place the mixture into the prepared baking dish and with the back of a spatula, smooth the top surface.
8. Select "Air Fry" of Breville Smart Air Fryer Oven and adjust the temperature to 355 degrees F.
9. Set the timer for 20 minutes and press "Start/Stop" to begin preheating.
10. When the unit beeps to show that it is preheated, arrange the baking dish over the wire rack.
11. When the cooking time is complete, remove the baking dish from oven and place onto a wire rack to cool completely.
12. Cut into 4 equal-sized squares and serve.

Fudge Brownies

Servings: 8
Preparation Time: 15 minutes
Cooking Time: 20 minutes

Ingredients:

- 1 cup sugar
- ½ cup butter, melted
- ½ cup flour
- 1/3 cup cocoa powder
- 1 teaspoon baking powder
- 2 eggs
- 1 teaspoon vanilla extract

Instructions:

1. Grease a baking dish.
2. In a large bowl, add the sugar and butter and whisk until light and fluffy.
3. Add the remaining ingredients and mix until well combined.
4. Place the mixture into the prepared baking dish and with the back of a spatula, smooth the top surface.
5. Select "Air Fry" of Breville Smart Air Fryer Oven and adjust the temperature to 350 degrees F.
6. Set the timer for 20 minutes and press "Start/Stop" to begin preheating.
7. When the unit beeps to show that it is preheated, arrange the baking dish over the wire rack.
8. When the cooking time is complete, remove the baking dish from oven and place onto a wire rack to cool completely.

9. Cut into 8 equal-sized squares and serve.

Strawberry Danish

Servings: 6
Preparation Time: 20 minutes
Cooking Time: 25 minutes

Ingredients:

- 1 tube full-sheet crescent roll dough
- 4 ounces cream cheese, softened
- ¼ cup strawberry jam
- ½ cup fresh strawberries, hulled and chopped
- 1 cup confectioner's sugar
- 2-3 tablespoons cream

Instructions:

1. Place the sheet of crescent roll dough onto a flat surface and unroll it.
2. In a microwave-safe bowl, add the cream cheese and microwave for about 20-30 seconds.
3. Remove from microwave and stir until creamy and smooth.
4. Spread the cream cheese over the dough sheet, followed by the strawberry jam.
5. Now, place the strawberry pieces evenly across the top.
6. From the short side, roll the dough and pinch the seam to seal.
7. Arrange a greased parchment paper into the enamel roasting pan.
8. Carefully curve the rolled pastry into a horseshoe shape and arrange into the prepared roasting pan.
9. Select "Air Fry" of Breville Smart Air Fryer Oven and adjust the temperature to 350 degrees F.
10. Set the timer for 25 minutes and press "Start/Stop" to begin preheating.
11. When the unit beeps to show that it is preheated, insert the roasting pan in the oven.
12. Flip the rolls once halfway through and spray with the cooking spray.
13. When the cooking time is complete, remove the roasting pan from the oven and place onto a rack to cool.
14. Meanwhile, in a bowl, mix together the confectioner's sugar and cream.
15. Drizzle the cream mixture over cooled Danish and serve.

Nutella Banana Muffins

Servings: 12
Preparation Time: 15 minutes
Cooking Time: 25 minutes

Ingredients:

- 1 2/3 cups plain flour
- 1 teaspoon baking soda
- 1 teaspoon baking powder
- 1 teaspoon ground cinnamon
- ¼ teaspoon salt
- 4 ripe bananas, peeled and mashed
- 2 eggs
- ½ cup brown sugar
- 1 teaspoon vanilla essence
- 3 tablespoons milk
- 1 tablespoon Nutella
- ¼ cup walnuts

Instructions:

1. Grease 12 muffin molds. Set aside.
2. In a large bowl, sift together the flour, baking soda, baking powder, cinnamon, and salt.
3. In another bowl, mix together the remaining ingredients except for walnuts.
4. Add the banana mixture into the flour mixture and mix until just combined.
5. Fold in the walnuts.
6. Place the mixture into the prepared muffin molds.
7. Select "Air Fry" of Breville Smart Air Fryer Oven and adjust the temperature to 250 degrees F.
8. Set the timer for 25 minutes and press "Start/Stop" to begin preheating.
9. When the unit beeps to show that it is preheated, arrange the muffin molds over the wire rack.
10. When the cooking time is complete, remove the muffin molds from oven and set aside to cool for about 10 minutes.
11. Carefully invert the muffins onto the wire rack to completely

Brownie Muffins

Servings: 12
Preparation Time: 10 minutes
Cooking Time: 10 minutes

Ingredients:

- 1 package Betty Crocker fudge brownie mix
- ¼ cup walnuts, chopped
- 1 egg
- 1/3 cup vegetable oil
- 2 teaspoons water

Instructions:

1. Grease 12 muffin melds. Set aside.
2. In a bowl, mix together all the ingredients.
3. Place the mixture into the prepared muffin molds.
4. Select "Air Fry" of Breville Smart Air Fryer Oven and adjust the temperature to 300 degrees F.
5. Set the timer for 10 minutes and press "Start/Stop" to begin preheating.
6. When the unit beeps to show that it is preheated, arrange the muffin molds over the wire rack.
7. When the cooking time is complete, remove the muffin molds from oven and set aside to cool for about 10 minutes.
8. Carefully invert the muffins onto the wire rack to completely

Strawberry Cupcakes

Servings: 10
Preparation Time: 20 minutes
Cooking Time: 8 minutes

Ingredients:

For Cupcakes

- ½ cup caster sugar
- 7 tablespoons butter
- 2 eggs
- ½ teaspoon vanilla essence
- 7/8 cup self-rising flour

For Frosting

- 1 cup icing sugar
- 3½ tablespoons butter
- 1 tablespoon whipped cream
- ¼ cup fresh strawberries, pureed
- ½ teaspoon pink food color

Instructions:

1. In a bowl, add the butter and sugar and beat until fluffy and light.
2. Add the eggs, one at a time and beat until well combined.
3. Stir in the vanilla extract.
4. Gradually, add the flour, beating continuously until well combined.
5. Place the mixture into 10 silicone cups.
6. Select "Air Fry" of Breville Smart Air Fryer Oven and adjust the temperature to 340 degrees F.
7. Set the timer for 8 minutes and press "Start/Stop" to begin preheating.
8. When the unit beeps to show that it is preheated, arrange the silicone cups over the wire rack.
9. When the cooking time is complete, remove the silicone cups from oven and set aside to cool for about 10 minutes.
10. Carefully invert the muffins onto the wire rack to completely cool before frosting.
11. For frosting: in a bowl, add the icing sugar and butter and whisk until fluffy and light.
12. Add the whipped cream, strawberry puree, and color and mix until well combined.
13. Fill the pastry bag with frosting and decorate the cupcakes

Red Velvet Cupcakes

Servings: 12
Preparation Time: 20 minutes
Cooking Time: 10 minutes

Ingredients:

For Cupcakes

- 2 cups refined flour
- ¾ cup icing sugar
- 2 teaspoons beet powder
- 1 teaspoon cocoa powder
- ¾ cup peanut butter
- 3 eggs

For Frosting

- 1 cup butter
- 1 (8-ounce) package cream cheese, softened
- 2 teaspoons vanilla extract

- ¼ teaspoon salt
- 4½ cups powdered sugar

For Garnishing

- ½ cup fresh raspberries

Instructions:

1. For cupcakes: in a bowl, add all the ingredients and with an electric whisker, whisk until well combined.
2. Place the mixture into silicone cups.
3. Select "Air Fry" of Breville Smart Air Fryer Oven and adjust the temperature to 340 degrees F.
4. Set the timer for 12 minutes and press "Start/Stop" to begin preheating.
5. When the unit beeps to show that it is preheated, arrange the silicone cups over the wire rack.
6. When the cooking time is complete, remove the silicone cups from oven and set aside to cool for about 10 minutes.
7. Carefully invert the cupcakes onto the wire rack to completely cool before frosting.
8. For frosting: in a large bowl, mix well butter, cream cheese, vanilla extract, and salt.
9. Add the powdered sugar, one cup at a time, whisking well after each addition.
10. Spread frosting evenly over each cupcake.
11. Garnish with raspberries and serve.

Banana Mug Cake

Servings: 1
Preparation Time: 10 minutes
Cooking Time: 30 minutes

Ingredients:

- ¼ cup all-purpose flour
- 1/8 teaspoon ground cinnamon
- ¼ teaspoon baking soda
- 1/8 teaspoon salt
- ½ cup banana, peeled and mashed
- 2 tablespoons sugar
- 1 tablespoon butter, melted
- 1 egg yolk
- ¼ teaspoon vanilla extract

Instructions:

1. In a bowl, mix together the flour, baking soda, cinnamon and salt.
2. In another bowl, add the mashed banana and sugar and beat well.
3. Add the butter, the egg yolk, and the vanilla and mix well.
4. Add the flour mixture and mix until just combined.
5. Place the mixture into a lightly greased ramekin.
6. Select "Air Fry" of Breville Smart Air Fryer Oven and adjust the temperature to 350 degrees F.
7. Set the timer for 30 minutes and press "Start/Stop" to begin preheating.
8. When the unit beeps to show that it is preheated, arrange the ramekin over the wire rack.
9. When the cooking time is complete, remove the ramekin from oven and set aside to cool slightly before serving.

Carrot Mug Cake

Serving: 1
Preparation Time: 15 minutes
Cooking Time: 20 minutes

Ingredients:

- ¼ cup whole-wheat pastry flour
- 1 tablespoon coconut sugar
- ¼ teaspoon baking powder
- 1/8 teaspoon ground cinnamon
- 1/8 teaspoon ground ginger
- Pinch of ground cloves
- Pinch of ground allspice
- Pinch of salt
- 2 tablespoons plus 2 teaspoons unsweetened almond milk
- 2 tablespoons carrot, peeled and grated
- 2 tablespoons walnuts, chopped
- 1 tablespoon raisins
- 2 teaspoons applesauce

Instructions:

1. In a bowl, mix together the flour, sugar, baking powder, spices and salt.
2. Add the remaining ingredients and mix until well combined.

3. Place the mixture into a lightly greased ramekin.
4. Select "Air Fry" of Breville Smart Air Fryer Oven and adjust the temperature to 350 degrees F.
5. Set the timer for 20 minutes and press "Start/Stop" to begin preheating.
6. When the unit beeps to show that it is preheated, arrange the ramekin over the wire rack.
7. When the cooking time is complete, remove the ramekin from oven and set aside to cool slightly before serving.

Chocolate Lava Cake

Servings: 4
Preparation Time: 10 minutes
Cooking Time: 9 minutes

Ingredients:

- 2/3 cup chocolate chips
- ½ cup unsalted butter, softened
- 2 large eggs
- 2 large egg yolks
- 1 cup confectioners' sugar
- 1 teaspoon peppermint extract
- 1/3 cup all-purpose flour plus more for dusting
- 2 tablespoons powdered sugar
- 1/3 cup fresh raspberries

Instructions:

1. Grease 4 ramekins and dust each with a little flour.
2. In a microwave-safe bowl, add the chocolate chips and butter. Microwave on high heat for about 30 seconds.
3. Remove the bowl from the microwave and stir the mixture well.
4. Add the eggs, egg yolks and confectioners' sugar and whisk until well combined.
5. Add the flour and gently stir to combine.
6. Place mixture into the prepared ramekins evenly.
7. Select "Air Fry" of Breville Smart Air Fryer Oven and adjust the temperature to 350 degrees F.
8. Set the timer for 40 minutes and press "Start/Stop" to begin preheating.
9. When the unit beeps to show that it is preheated, arrange the ramekins over the wire rack.
10. When the cooking time is complete, remove the ramekins from oven and set aside to cool

completely before serving and place onto a wire rack to cool for about 5 minutes.
11. Carefully run a knife around the sides of each ramekin several times to loosen the cake.
12. Carefully invert each cake onto a dessert plate and dust with powdered sugar.
13. Garnish with raspberries and serve immediately.

Butter Cake

Servings: 6
Preparation Time: 15 minutes
Cooking Time: 15 minutes

Ingredients:

- 3 ounces butter, softened
- ½ cup caster sugar
- 1 egg
- 1 1/3 cups plain flour, sifted
- Pinch of salt
- ½ cup milk
- 1 tablespoon icing sugar

Instructions:

1. In a bowl, add the butter and sugar and whisk until light and creamy.
2. Add the egg and whisk until smooth and fluffy.
3. Add the flour and salt and mix well alternately with the milk.
4. Grease a small Bundt cake pan.
5. Place mixture evenly into the prepared cake pan.
6. Select "Air Fry" of Breville Smart Air Fryer Oven and adjust the temperature to 350 degrees F.
7. Set the timer for 15 minutes and press "Start/Stop" to begin preheating.
8. When the unit beeps to show that it is preheated, arrange the cake pan over the wire rack.
9. When the cooking time is complete, remove the cake pan from oven and place onto a wire rack to cool for about 10 minutes.
10. Carefully invert the cake onto the wire rack to completely cool before slicing.
11. Just before serving, dust the cake with icing sugar.
12. Cut into desired sized slices and serve.

Rum Cake

Servings: 6
Preparation Time: 15 minutes
Cooking Time: 25 minutes

Ingredients:

- ½ package yellow cake mix
- ½ (3.4-ounce) package Jell-O instant pudding
- 2 eggs
- ¼ cup vegetable oil
- ¼ cup water
- ¼ cup dark rum

Instructions:

1. In a bowl, add all the ingredients and with an electric mixer, beat until well combined.
2. Arrange a parchment paper in the bottom of a greased 8-inch pan.
3. Now, arrange a foil piece around the cake pan.
4. Place the mixture into the prepared cake pan and with the back of a spoon, smooth the top surface.
5. Select "Air Fry" of Breville Smart Air Fryer Oven and adjust the temperature to 325 degrees F.
6. Set the timer for 25 minutes and press "Start/Stop" to begin preheating.
7. When the unit beeps to show that it is preheated, arrange the cake pan over the wire rack.
8. When the cooking time is complete, remove the cake pan from oven and place onto a wire rack to cool for about 10 minutes.
9. Carefully invert the cake onto the wire rack to cool completely before cutting.
10. Cut into desired-sized slices and serve.

Chocolate Cream Cake

Servings: 6
Preparation Time: 15 minutes
Cooking Time: 25 minutes

Ingredients:

- 1 cup flour
- 1/3 cup cocoa powder
- 1 teaspoon baking powder
- ½ teaspoon baking soda

- 1/8 teaspoon salt
- 3 eggs
- 2/3 cup sugar
- ½ cup sour cream
- ½ cup butter, softened
- 2 teaspoons vanilla extract

Instructions:

1. In a large bowl, mix together the flour, cocoa powder, baking powder, baking soda, and salt.
2. Add the remaining ingredients and with an electric whisker, whisk on low speed until well combined.
3. Place the mixture evenly into a lightly greased cake pan.
4. Select "Air Fry" of Breville Smart Air Fryer Oven and adjust the temperature to 320 degrees F.
5. Set the timer for 25 minutes and press "Start/Stop" to begin preheating.
6. When the unit beeps to show that it is preheated, arrange the cake pan over the wire rack.
7. When the cooking time is complete, remove the cake pan from oven and place onto a wire rack to cool for about 10 minutes.
8. Carefully invert the cake onto the wire rack to completely cool before slicing.
9. Cut the cake into desired-sized slices and serve.

Semolina Cake

Servings: 6
Preparation Time: 15 minutes
Cooking Time: 15 minutes

Ingredients:

- 2½ cups semolina
- ½ cup vegetable oil
- 1 cup milk
- 1 cup plain Greek yogurt
- 1 cup sugar
- ½ teaspoon baking soda
- 1½ teaspoons baking powder
- Pinch of salt
- ¼ cup raisins
- ¼ cup walnuts, chopped

Instructions:

1. In a bowl, mix together the semolina, oil, milk, yogurt, and sugar.
2. Cover the bowl and set aside for about 15 minutes.
3. In the bowl f semolina mixture, add the baking soda, baking powder, and salt in the bowl of semolina mixture and mix until well combined.
4. Fold in the raisins and walnuts.
5. Place the mixture into a lightly greased cake pan.
6. Select "Air Fry" of Breville Smart Air Fryer Oven and adjust the temperature to 320 degrees F.
7. Set the timer for 15 minutes and press "Start/Stop" to begin preheating.
8. When the unit beeps to show that it is preheated, arrange the cake pan over the wire rack.
9. When the cooking time is complete, remove the cake pan from oven and place onto a wire rack to cool for about 10 minutes.
10. Carefully invert the cake onto the wire rack to completely cool before slicing.
11. Cut the cake into desired-sized slices and serve.

Mini Cheesecakes

Servings: 4
Preparation Time: 10 minutes
Cooking Time: 10 minutes

Ingredients:

- ¾ cup sugar
- 2 eggs
- 1 teaspoon vanilla extract
- ½ teaspoon fresh lime juice
- 16 ounces cream cheese, softened
- 2 tablespoon heavy cream

Instructions:

1. In a blender, add the sugar, eggs, vanilla extract and lime juice and pulse until smooth.
2. Add the cream cheese and sour cream and pulse until smooth.
3. Place the mixture into 2 (4-inch) springform pans evenly.
4. Arrange the ramekins onto the enamel roasting pan.
5. Select "Air Fry" of Breville Smart Air Fryer Oven and adjust the temperature to 350 degrees F.
6. Set the timer for 10 minutes and press "Start/Stop" to begin preheating.
7. When the unit beeps to show that it is preheated, insert the roasting pan in the oven.
8. When the cooking time is complete, remove the roasting pan from the oven.
9. Place the ramekins onto a wire rack to cool.
10. Refrigerate overnight before serving.

Vanilla Cheesecake

Servings: 6
Preparation Time: 15 minutes
Cooking Time: 14 minutes

Ingredients:

- 1 cup honey graham cracker crumbs
- 2 tablespoons unsalted butter, softened
- 1 pound cream cheese, softened
- ½ cup sugar
- 2 large eggs
- ½ teaspoon vanilla extract

Instructions:

1. Line a round baking pan with parchment paper.
2. For crust: in a bowl, add the graham cracker crumbs and butter.
3. Place the crust into the baking dish and press to smooth.
4. Select "Air Fry" of Breville Smart Air Fryer Oven and adjust the temperature to 350 degrees F.
5. Set the timer for 4 minutes and press "Start/Stop" to begin preheating.
6. When the unit beeps to show that it is preheated, insert the baking pan in the oven.
7. When the cooking time is complete, remove the baking pan from the oven and set aside to cool for about 10 minutes.
8. Meanwhile, in a bowl, add the cream cheese and sugar and whisk until smooth.
9. Now, place the eggs, one at a time and whisk until the mixture becomes creamy.
10. Add the vanilla extract and mix well.
11. Place the cream cheese mixture evenly over the crust.
12. Select "Air Fry" of Breville Smart Air Fryer Oven and adjust the temperature to 350 degrees F.
13. Set the timer for 10 minutes and press "Start/Stop" to begin preheating.

14. When the unit beeps to show that it is preheated, insert the baking pan in the oven.
15. When the cooking time is complete, remove the baking pan from the oven and set aside to cool completely.
16. Refrigerate overnight before serving.

Ricotta Cheesecake

Servings: 8
Preparation Time: 15 minutes
Cooking Time: 25 minutes

Ingredients:

- 17.6 ounces ricotta cheese
- 3 eggs
- ¾ cup sugar
- 3 tablespoons corn starch
- 1 tablespoon fresh lemon juice
- 2 teaspoons vanilla extract
- 1 teaspoon fresh lemon zest, finely grated

Instructions:

1. In a large bowl, place all ingredients and mix until well combined.
2. Place the mixture into a cake pan.
3. Select "Air Fry" of Breville Smart Air Fryer Oven and adjust the temperature to 320 degrees F.
4. Set the timer for 25 minutes and press "Start/Stop" to begin preheating.
5. When the unit beeps to show that it is preheated, arrange the cake pan over the wire rack.
6. When the cooking time is complete, remove the cake pan from oven and place onto a wire rack to cool completely.
7. Refrigerate overnight before serving.

Pecan Pie

Servings: 5
Preparation Time: 15 minutes
Cooking Time: 35 minutes

Ingredients:

- ¾ cup brown sugar
- ¼ cup caster sugar

- 1/3 cup butter, melted
- 2 large eggs
- 1¾ tablespoons flour
- 1 tablespoon milk
- 1 teaspoon vanilla extract
- 1 cup pecan halves
- 1 frozen pie crust, thawed

Instructions:

1. In a large bowl, mix together the sugars and butter.
2. Add the eggs and whisk until foamy.
3. Add the flour, milk, and vanilla extract and whisk until well combined.
4. Fold in the pecan halves.
5. Grease a pie pan.
6. Arrange the crust in the bottom of the prepared pie pan.
7. Place the pecan mixture over the crust evenly.
8. Select "Air Fry" of Breville Smart Air Fryer Oven and adjust the temperature to 300 degrees F.
9. Set the timer for 22 minutes and press "Start/Stop" to begin preheating.
10. When the unit beeps to show that it is preheated, place the pie pan over the wire rack.
11. After 22 minutes of cooking, to set the temperature at 385 degrees F for 13 minutes.
12. When the cooking time is complete, remove the air fry basket from the oven and place the pie pan onto a wire rack to cool for about 10-15 minutes before serving.

Blueberry Cobbler

Servings: 6
Preparation Time: 15 minutes
Cooking Time: 20 minutes

Ingredients:

For Filling:

- 2½ cups fresh blueberries
- 1 teaspoon vanilla extract
- 1 teaspoon fresh lemon juice
- 1 cup sugar
- 1 teaspoon flour
- 1 tablespoon butter, melted

For Topping:

- 1¾ cups all-purpose flour
- 6 tablespoons sugar
- 4 teaspoons baking powder
- 1 cup milk
- 5 tablespoons butter

For Sprinkling:

- 2 teaspoons sugar
- ¼ teaspoon ground cinnamon

Instructions:

1. For filling: in a bowl, add all the ingredients and mix until well combined.
2. In another large bowl, mix together the flour, baking powder, and sugar.
3. Add the milk and butter and mix until a crumbly mixture forms.
4. For sprinkling: in a small bowl, mix together the sugar and cinnamon.
5. In the bottom of a greased cake pan, place the blueberries mixture and top with the flour mixture evenly.
6. Sprinkle the cinnamon sugar on top evenly.
7. Select "Air Fry" of Breville Smart Air Fryer Oven and adjust the temperature to 320 degrees F.
8. Set the timer for 20 minutes and press "Start/Stop" to begin preheating.
9. When the unit beeps to show that it is preheated, arrange the cake pan over the wire rack.
10. When the cooking time is complete, remove the cake pan from oven and place onto a wire rack to cool for about 10 minutes before serving.

Plum Crisp

Servings: 2
Preparation Time: 15 minutes
Cooking Time: 40 minutes

Ingredients:

- 1½ cups plums, pitted and sliced
- ¼ cup sugar, divided
- 1½ teaspoons cornstarch
- 3 tablespoons flour

- ¼ teaspoon ground cinnamon
- Pinch of salt
- 1½ tablespoons cold butter, chopped
- 3 tablespoons rolled oats

Instructions:

1. In a bowl, place plum slices, 1 teaspoon of sugar and cornstarch and toss to coat well.
2. Divide the plum mixture into lightly greased 2 (8-ounce) ramekins.
3. In a bowl, mix together the flour, remaining sugar, cinnamon and salt.
4. With a pastry blender, cut in bitterer until a crumbly mixture forms.
5. Add the oats and gently stir to combine.
6. Place the oat mixture over plum slices into each ramekin.
7. Select "Bake" of Breville Smart Air Fryer Oven and adjust the temperature to 350 degrees F.
8. Set the timer for 40 minutes and press "Start/Stop" to begin preheating.
9. When the unit beeps to show that it is preheated, arrange the ramekins over the wire rack.
10. When the cooking time is complete, remove the ramekins from oven and set aside to cool completely before serving and place onto a wire rack to cool for about 10 minutes.
11. Serve warm.

Fruity Crumble

Servings: 4
Preparation Time: 15minutes
Cooking Time: 20 minutes

Ingredients:

- ½ pound fresh apricots, pitted and cubed
- 1 cup fresh blackberries
- 1/3 cup sugar, divided
- 1 tablespoon fresh lemon juice
- 7/8 cup flour
- Pinch of salt
- 1 tablespoon cold water
- ¼ cup chilled butter, cubed

Instructions:

1. Grease a baking dish.

2. In a large bowl, mix together the apricots, blackberries, 2 tablespoons of sugar, and lemon juice.
3. Spread the apricot mixture into the prepared baking dish.
4. In another bowl, add the flour, remaining sugar, salt, water, and butter and mix until a crumbly mixture forms.
5. Spread the flour mixture over the apricot mixture evenly.
6. Select "Air Fry" of Breville Smart Air Fryer Oven and adjust the temperature to 390 degrees F.
7. Set the timer for 20 minutes and press "Start/Stop" to begin preheating.
8. When the unit beeps to show that it is preheated, arrange the baking dish over the wire rack.
9. When the cooking time is complete, remove the baking dish from oven and place onto a wire rack to cool for about 10 minutes before serving.
10. Serve warm.

Cherry Clafoutis

Servings: 4
Preparation Time: 15 minutes
Cooking Time: 25 minutes

Ingredients:

- 1½ cups fresh cherries, pitted
- 3 tablespoons vodka
- ¼ cup flour
- 2 tablespoons sugar
- Pinch of salt
- ½ cup sour cream
- 1 egg
- 1 tablespoon butter
- ¼ cup powdered sugar

Instructions:

1. In a bowl, mix together the cherries and vodka.
2. In another bowl, mix together the flour, sugar, and salt.
3. Add the sour cream and egg and mix until a smooth dough forms.
4. Grease a cake pan.
5. Place flour mixture evenly into the prepared cake pan.
6. Spread cherry mixture over the dough.
7. Place butter on top in the form of dots.

8. Select "Air Fry" of Breville Smart Air Fryer Oven and adjust the temperature to 355 degrees F.
9. Set the timer for 25 minutes and press "Start/Stop" to begin preheating.
10. When the unit beeps to show that it is preheated, arrange the cake pan over the wire rack.
11. When the cooking time is complete, remove the cake pan from oven and place onto a wire rack to cool for about 10-15 minutes before serving.
12. Now, invert the Clafoutis onto a platter and sprinkle with powdered sugar.
13. Cut the Clafoutis into desired size slices and serve warm.

Raisin Bread Pudding

Servings: 3
Preparation Time: 15 minutes
Cooking Time: 12 minutes

Ingredients:

- 1 cup milk
- 1 egg
- 1 tablespoon brown sugar
- ½ teaspoon ground cinnamon
- ¼ teaspoon vanilla extract
- 2 tablespoons raisins, soaked in hot water for about 15 minutes
- 2 bread slices, cut into small cubes
- 1 tablespoon chocolate chips
- 1 tablespoon sugar

Instructions:

1. In a bowl, mix together the milk, egg, brown sugar, cinnamon, and vanilla extract.
2. Stir in the raisins.
3. In a baking dish, spread the bread cubes and top evenly with the milk mixture.
4. Refrigerate for about 15-20 minutes.
5. Select "Air Fry" of Breville Smart Air Fryer Oven and adjust the temperature to 375 degrees F.
6. Set the timer for 12 minutes and press "Start/Stop" to begin preheating.
7. When the unit beeps to show that it is preheated, arrange the baking dish over the wire rack.
8. When the cooking time is complete, remove the baking dish from oven and place onto a wire rack to cool for about 10 minutes before serving.
9. Serve warm.

Donuts Pudding

Servings: 6
Preparation Time: 15 minutes
Cooking Time: 1 hour

Ingredients:

- 6 glazed donuts, cut into small pieces
- ¾ cup frozen sweet cherries
- ½ cup raisins
- ½ cup semi-sweet chocolate baking chips
- ¼ cup sugar
- 1 teaspoon ground cinnamon
- 4 egg yolks
- 1½ cups whipping cream

Instructions:

1. In a large bowl, mix together the donut pieces, cherries, raisins, chocolate chips, sugar, and cinnamon.
2. In another bowl, add the egg yolks and whipping cream and whisk until well combined.
3. Add the egg yolk mixture into the doughnut mixture and mix well.
4. Line a baking dish with a piece of foil.
5. Place the donuts mixture into the prepared baking dish.
6. Select "Air Fry" of Breville Smart Air Fryer Oven and adjust the temperature to 360 degrees F.
7. Set the timer for 60 minutes and press "Start/Stop" to begin preheating.
8. When the unit beeps to show that it is preheated, arrange the baking dish over the wire rack.
9. When the cooking time is complete, remove the baking dish from oven and place onto a wire rack to cool for about 10–15 minutes before serving.
10. Serve warm.

Egg Soufflé

Servings: 6
Preparation Time: 15 minutes
Cooking Time: 30 minutes

Ingredients:

- ¼ cup butter, softened
- ¼ cup all-purpose flour
- ½ cup plus 2 tablespoons sugar, divided
- 1 cup milk
- 3 teaspoons vanilla extract, divided
- 4 egg yolks
- 5 egg whites
- 1 teaspoon cream of tartar
- 2 tablespoons powdered sugar plus extra for dusting

Instructions:

1. In a bowl, add the butter and flour and mix until smooth paste forms.
2. In a medium pan, mix together ½ cup of sugar and milk over medium-low heat and cook for about 3 minutes or until the sugar is dissolved, stirring continuously.
3. Add the flour mixture, whisking continuously and simmer for about 3-4 minutes or until the mixture becomes thick.
4. Remove from the heat and stir in 1 teaspoon of vanilla extract.
5. Set aside for about 10 minutes to cool.
6. In a bowl, mix together the egg yolks and 1 teaspoon of vanilla extract.
7. Add the egg yolk mixture into milk mixture and mix until well combined.
8. In another bowl, add the egg whites, cream of tartar, remaining sugar, and vanilla extract and whisk until stiff peaks form.
9. Fold the egg whites mixture into the milk mixture.
10. Place mixture into 6 greased ramekins evenly and with the back of a spoon, smooth the top surface.
11. Select "Air Fry" of Breville Smart Air Fryer Oven and adjust the temperature to 330 degrees F.
12. Set the timer for 16 minutes and press "Start/Stop" to begin preheating.
13. When the unit beeps to show that it is preheated, arrange the ramekins over the wire rack.
14. When the cooking time is complete, remove the ramekins from the oven and place onto a wire rack to cool slightly.
15. Sprinkle with the powdered sugar and serve warm.

Chocolate Soufflé

Servings: 2
Preparation Time: 15 minutes
Cooking Time: 16 minutes

Ingredients:

- 3 ounces semi-sweet chocolate, chopped
- ¼ cup butter
- 2 eggs, yolks and whites separated
- 3 tablespoons sugar
- ½ teaspoon pure vanilla extract
- 2 tablespoons all-purpose flour
- 1 teaspoon powdered sugar plus extra for dusting

Instructions:

1. In a microwave-safe bowl, place the butter and chocolate. Microwave on high heat for about 2 minutes or until melted completely, stirring after every 30 seconds.
2. Remove from the microwave and stir the mixture until smooth.
3. In another bowl, add the egg yolks and whisk well.
4. Add the sugar and vanilla extract and whisk well.
5. Add the chocolate mixture and mix until well combined.
6. Add the flour and mix well.
7. In a clean glass bowl, add the egg whites and whisk until soft peaks form.
8. Fold the whipped egg whites in 3 portions into the chocolate mixture.
9. Grease 2 ramekins and sprinkle each with a pinch of sugar.
10. Place mixture into the prepared ramekins and with the back of a spoon, smooth the top surface.
11. Select "Air Fry" of Breville Smart Air Fryer Oven and adjust the temperature to 330 degrees F.
12. Set the timer for 14 minutes and press "Start/Stop" to begin preheating.
13. When the unit beeps to show that it is preheated, arrange the ramekins over the wire rack.
14. When the cooking time is complete, remove the ramekins from oven and set aside to cool completely before serving and place onto a wire rack to cool slightly.
15. Sprinkle with the powdered sugar and serve warm.

Lemon Mousse

Servings: 2
Preparation Time: 10 minutes
Cooking Time: 12 minutes

Ingredients:

- 4 ounces cream cheese, softened
- ½ cup heavy cream
- 2 tablespoon fresh lemon juice
- 4-6 drops liquid stevia
- 2 pinches salt

Instructions:

1. In a bowl, add all the ingredients and mix until well combined.
2. Transfer the mixture into 2 ramekins.
3. Select "Bake" of Breville Smart Air Fryer Oven and adjust the temperature to 350 degrees F.
4. Set the timer for 12 minutes and press "Start/Stop" to begin preheating.
5. When the unit beeps to show that it is preheated, arrange the ramekins over the wire rack.
6. When the cooking time is complete, remove the ramekins from oven and set aside to cool completely before serving and place onto a wire rack to cool.
7. Refrigerate for at least 3 hours before serving.

Chocolate Pudding

Servings: 4
Preparation Time: 15 minutes
Cooking Time: 12 minutes

Ingredients:

- ½ cup butter
- 2/3 cup dark chocolate, chopped
- ¼ cup caster sugar
- 2 medium eggs
- 2 teaspoons fresh orange rind, finely grated
- ¼ cup fresh orange juice
- 2 tablespoons self-rising flour

Instructions:

1. In a microwave-safe bowl, add the butter and chocolate and microwave on high heat for about 2 minutes or until melted completely, stirring after every 30 seconds.
2. Remove from the microwave and stir the mixture until smooth.
3. Add the sugar and eggs and whisk until frothy.
4. Add the orange rind and juice, followed by flour and mix until well combined.
5. Divide mixture into 4 greased ramekins about ¾ full.
6. Select "Air Fry" of Breville Smart Air Fryer Oven and adjust the temperature to 355 degrees F.
7. Set the timer for 12 minutes and press "Start/Stop" to begin preheating.
8. When the unit beeps to show that it is preheated, arrange the ramekins over the wire rack.
9. When the cooking time is complete, remove the ramekins from oven and set aside to cool completely before serving.

Blueberry Custard

Servings: 6
Preparation Time: 15 minutes
Cooking Time: 3 hours

Ingredients:

- 6 large eggs, separated
- 2 cups light cream
- ½ cup coconut flour
- ½ cup sugar
- 1/3 cup fresh lemon juice
- 2 teaspoons lemon zest, grated
- 1 teaspoon lemon liquid stevia
- ½ teaspoon salt
- ½ cup fresh blueberries

Instructions:

1. Lightly grease an oven-safe pan that will fit in the Breville Smart Air Fryer Oven.
2. In the bowl of a stand mixer, add the egg whites and beat until stiff peaks form. Set aside.
3. In another bowl, add the egg yolks and remaining ingredients except for blueberries and beat until well combined.

4. Slowly add the whipped egg whites, a little at a time and gently, mix until just combined.
5. Place the mixture into the prepared pan and sprinkle with the blueberries.
6. Cover the pan with a lid.
7. Arrange the pan over the wire rack.
8. Select "Slow Cooker" of Breville Smart Air Fryer Oven and set on "High".
9. Set the timer for 3 hours and press "Start/Stop" to begin cooking.
10. When the cooking time is complete, remove the pan from the oven.
11. Remove the lid and transfer the custard into a large bowl.
12. Set aside to cool.
13. Refrigerate for about 2 hours before serving.

Chocolate Fondue

Servings: 8
Preparation Time: 10 minutes
Cooking Time: 1 hour

Ingredients:

- 6 ounces dark chocolate, chopped
- 1 cup heavy cream
- 1 ounce brewed coffee
- ½ cup sugar
- ¼ teaspoon liquid stevia
- 1 teaspoon vanilla extract

Instructions:

1. Line an oven-safe pan that will fit in the Breville Smart Air Fryer Oven with a greased parchment paper.
2. In the pan, place all the ingredients and stir to combine.
3. Cover the pan with a lid.
4. Arrange the pan over the wire rack.
5. Select "Slow Cooker" of Breville Smart Air Fryer Oven and set on "Low".
6. Set the timer for 1 hour and press "Start/Stop" to begin cooking.
7. When the cooking time is complete, remove the pan from the oven.
8. Remove the lid and with a wire whisk, mix until smooth.
9. Serve warm.

Conclusion

The Breville Smart Air Fryer Oven will help you cook everything that you want to serve at the table. Whether you are serving a large family gathering or cooking food, your homies, this kitchen miracle will help you cook all the portion sizes in just a few minutes. So, to buy all the different cooking appliances when you can replace them all with a single appliance which is simple to use and efficient in working. And if you have already made up your mind about the Breville Smart Air Fryer Oven, then this cookbook can be your perfect cooking partner as it will give you all the smart cooking secrets that you need to use this machine up to its full potential.

Made in the USA
Las Vegas, NV
13 November 2024

90577372-057d-40e2-83fa-4594fc896452R01